I0471566

# The Elements of Art
## Creating with Linear and Friends

by Kem Kowa

**DORRANCE**
PUBLISHING CO
EST. 1920
PITTSBURGH, PENNSYLVANIA 15238

Dorrance Publishing Co
585 Alpha Drive
Suite 103
Pittsburgh, PA 15238
Visit our website at *www.dorrancebookstore.com*

ISBN: 978-1-6453-0633-7
eISBN: 978-1-6453-0719-8

# The Elements of Art

## Creating with Linear and Friends

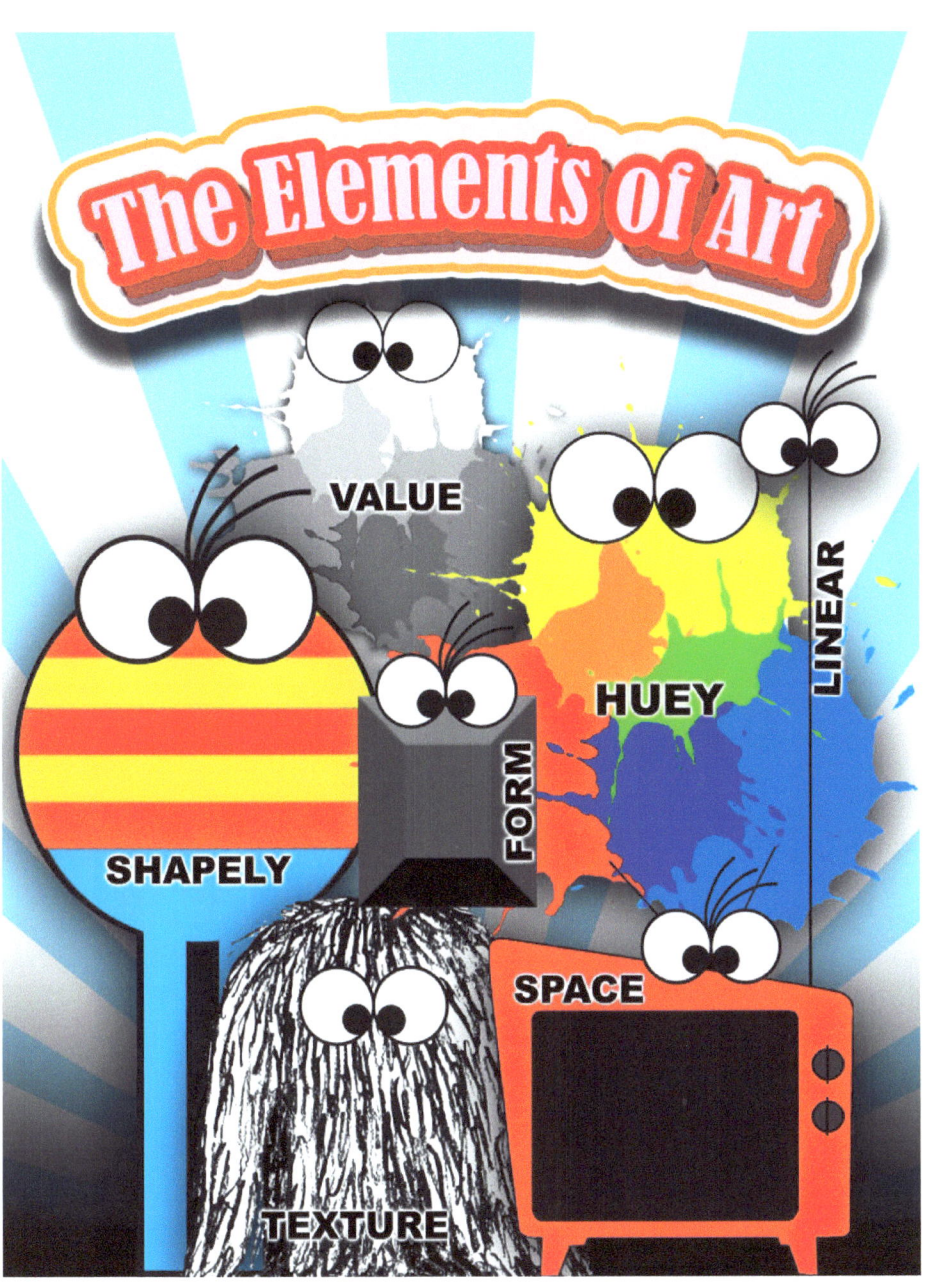

# INTRODUCTION

The lesson plans presented are designed to help children and adults see the world differently as they learn to fill their space using the elements of art.

Katherine "Kem" Kowa Author/Sponsor
Dinett Hok Co Author/Graphic Designer
Tom Shutters Video Production/Graphic Designer

# TABLE OF CONTENTS

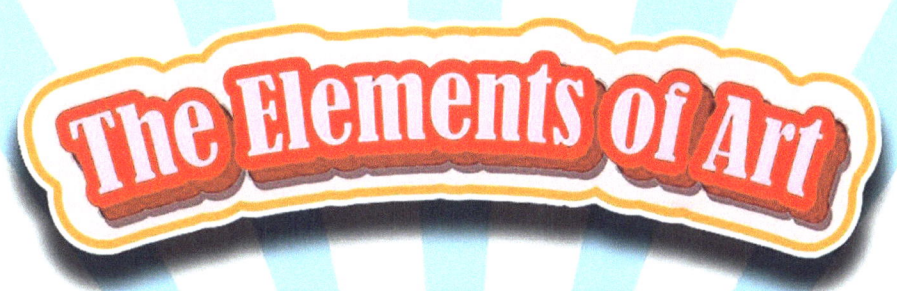

The Elements of Art are the individual parts that we use to create an artwork. Without the Elements of Art there is no artwork.

**1- Line**

**2- Shape**

**3- Form**

**4- Texture**

**5- Color**

**6- Value**

**7- Space**

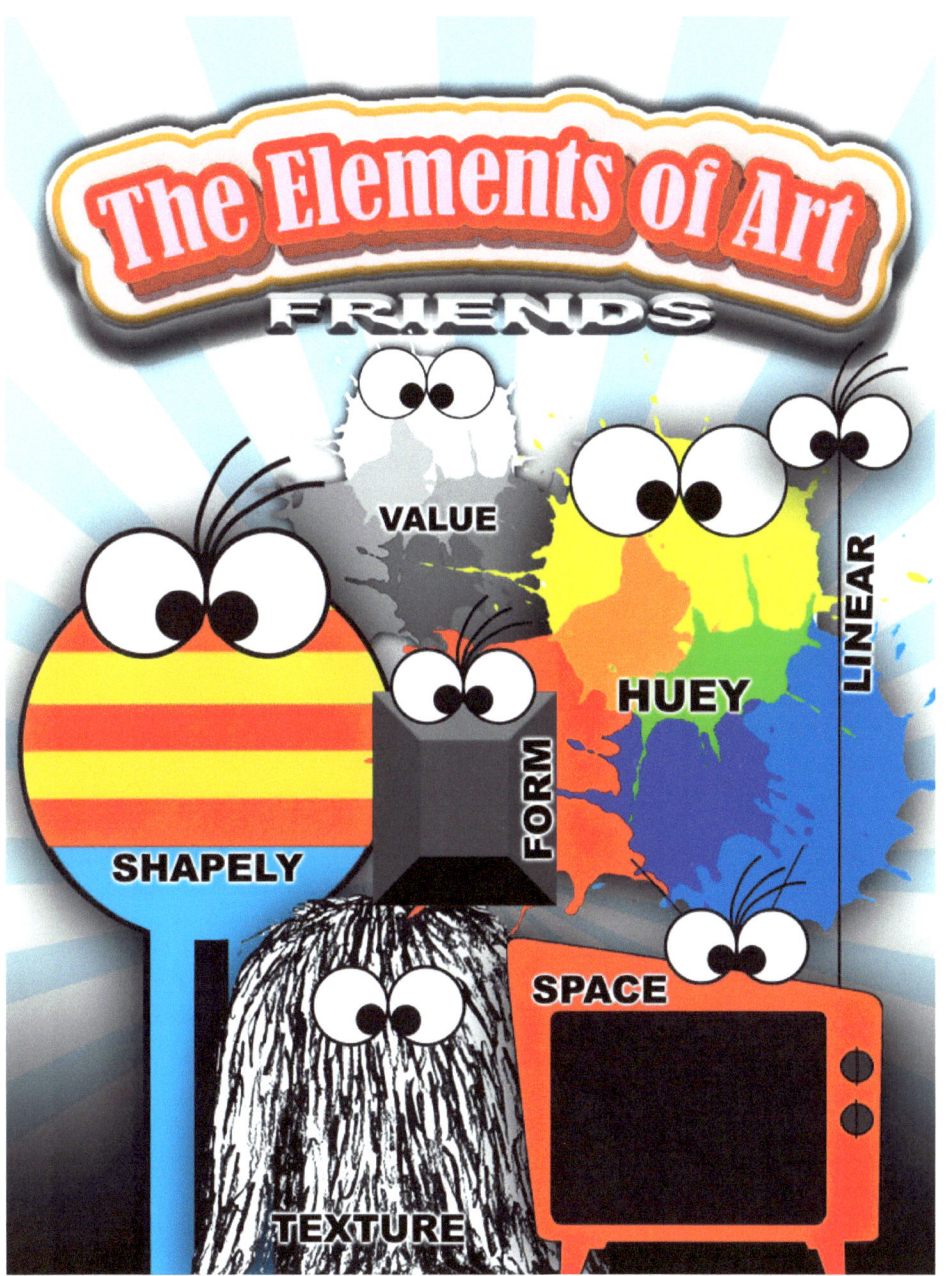

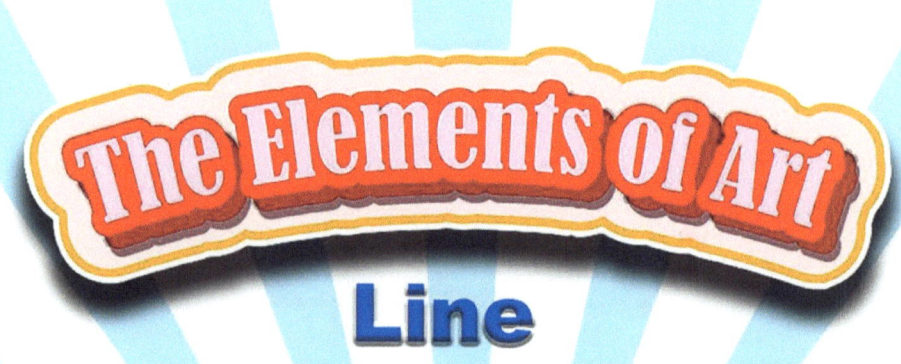

# Line

Line is the first Element of Art. A line starts with a dot or a mark moving in a space or surface. There are different types of lines.

**STRAIGHT**　　**SOFT**

**VERTICAL**　　**ZIGZAG**

**HORIZONTAL**　**WAVY**

**DOTTED**　　**SWIRL**

**THICK**　　　**SHADE**

**THIN**　　　**DASHED**

# The Elements of Art

## LESSON ONE
### Line

Supplies needed: drawing pad and pencils/markers.

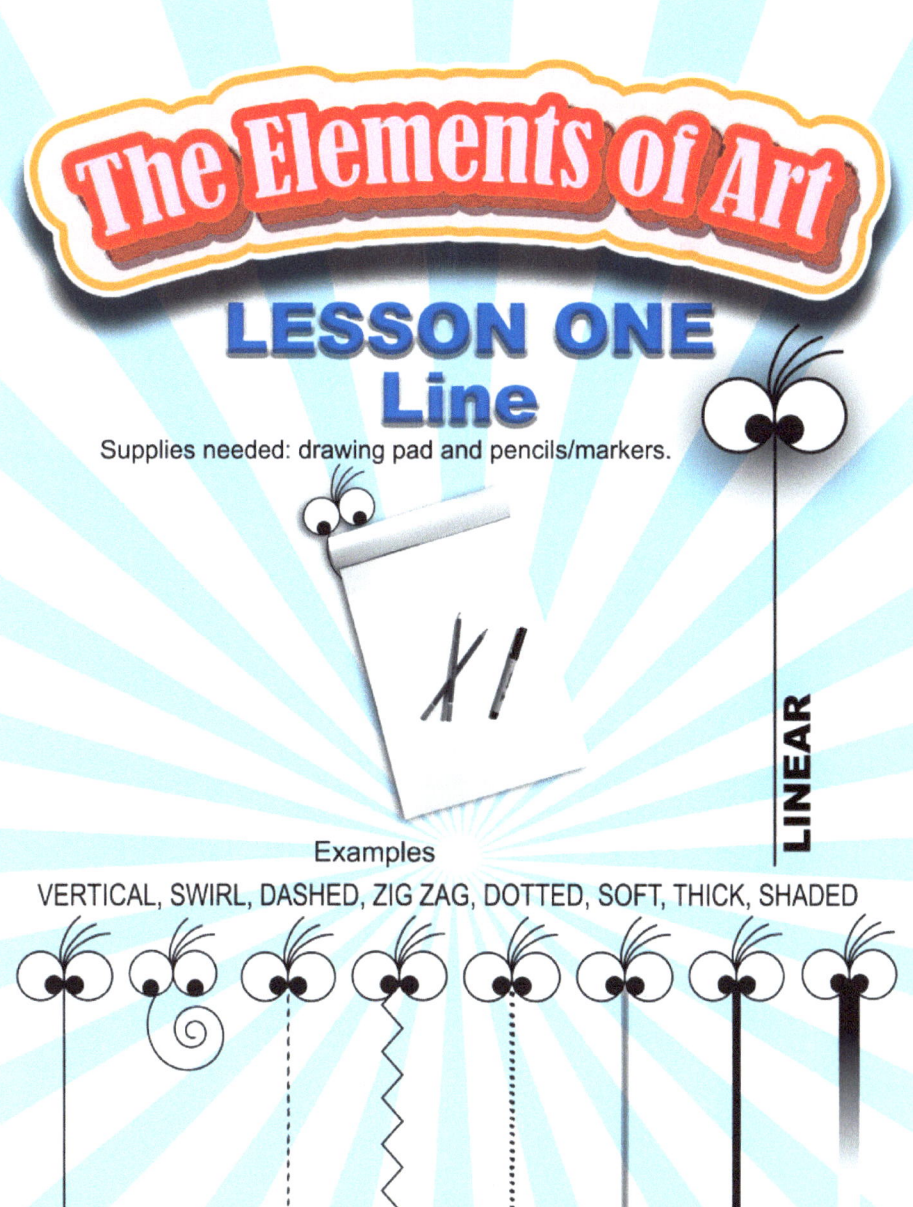

LINEAR

Examples

VERTICAL, SWIRL, DASHED, ZIG ZAG, DOTTED, SOFT, THICK, SHADED

# The Elements of Art

## LESSON ONE
## Line

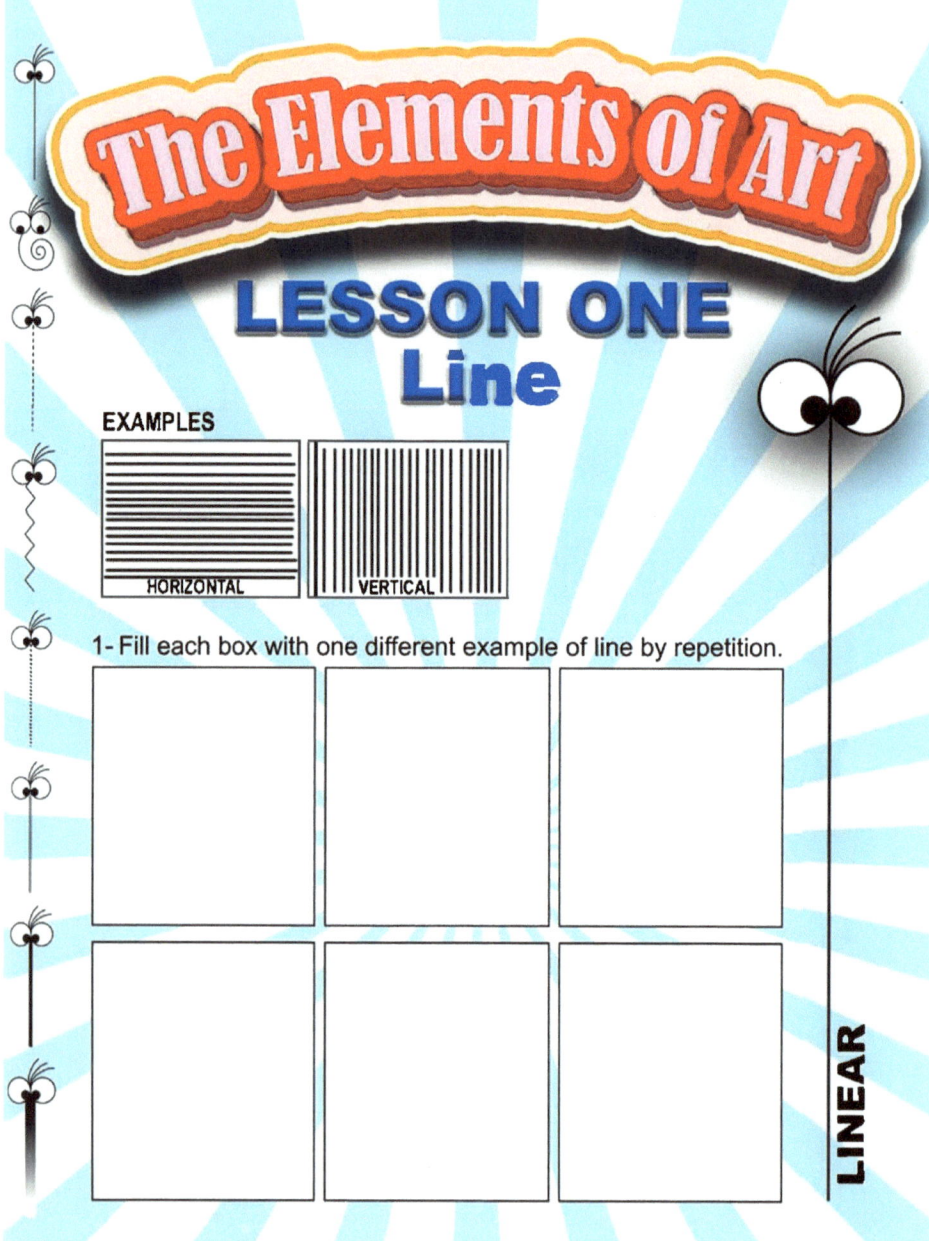

**EXAMPLES**

HORIZONTAL

VERTICAL

1- Fill each box with one different example of line by repetition.

LINEAR

# The Elements of Art

## LESSON ONE
## Line

EXAMPLES

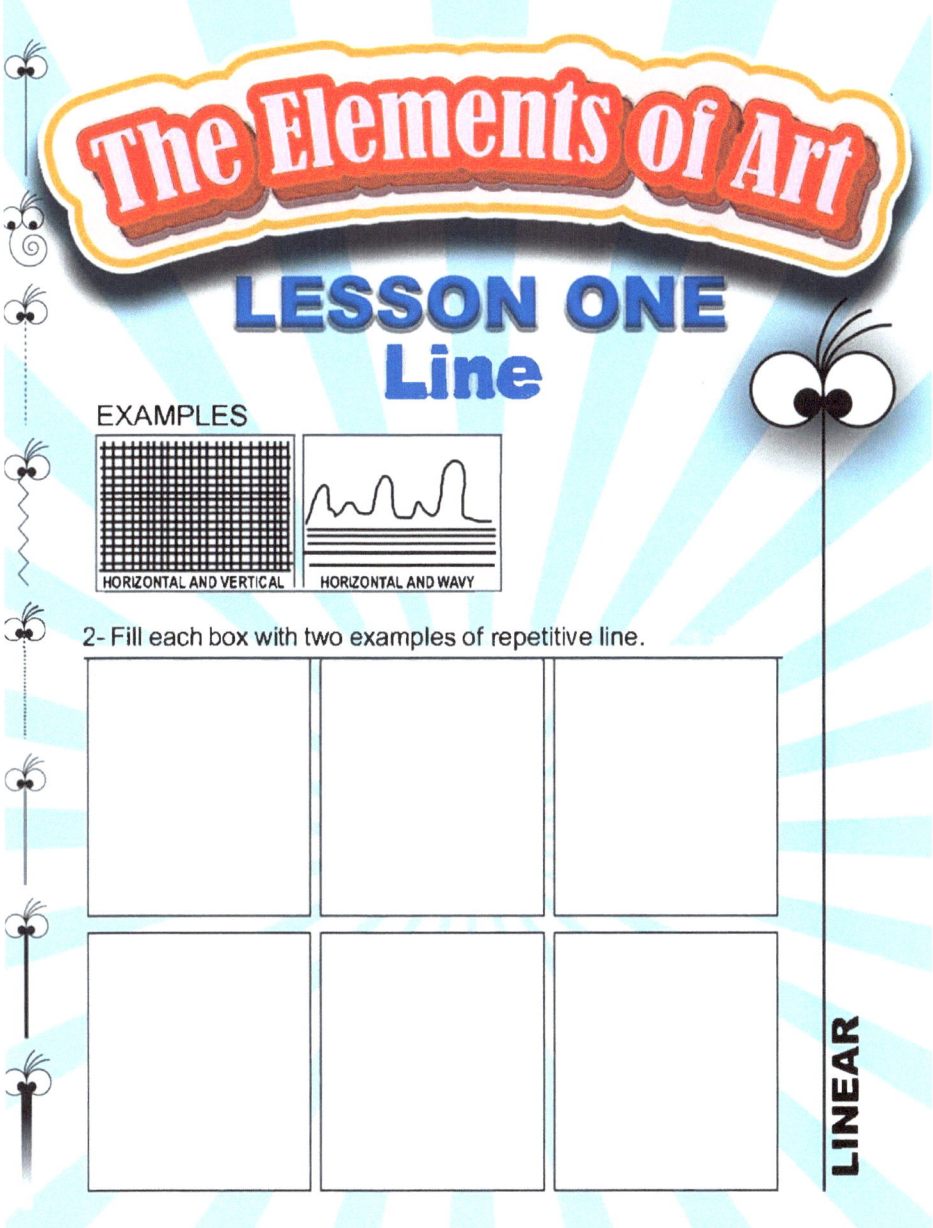

HORIZONTAL AND VERTICAL | HORIZONTAL AND WAVY

2- Fill each box with two examples of repetitive line.

LINEAR

# The Elements of Art

## LESSON ONE
### Line

**EXAMPLES**

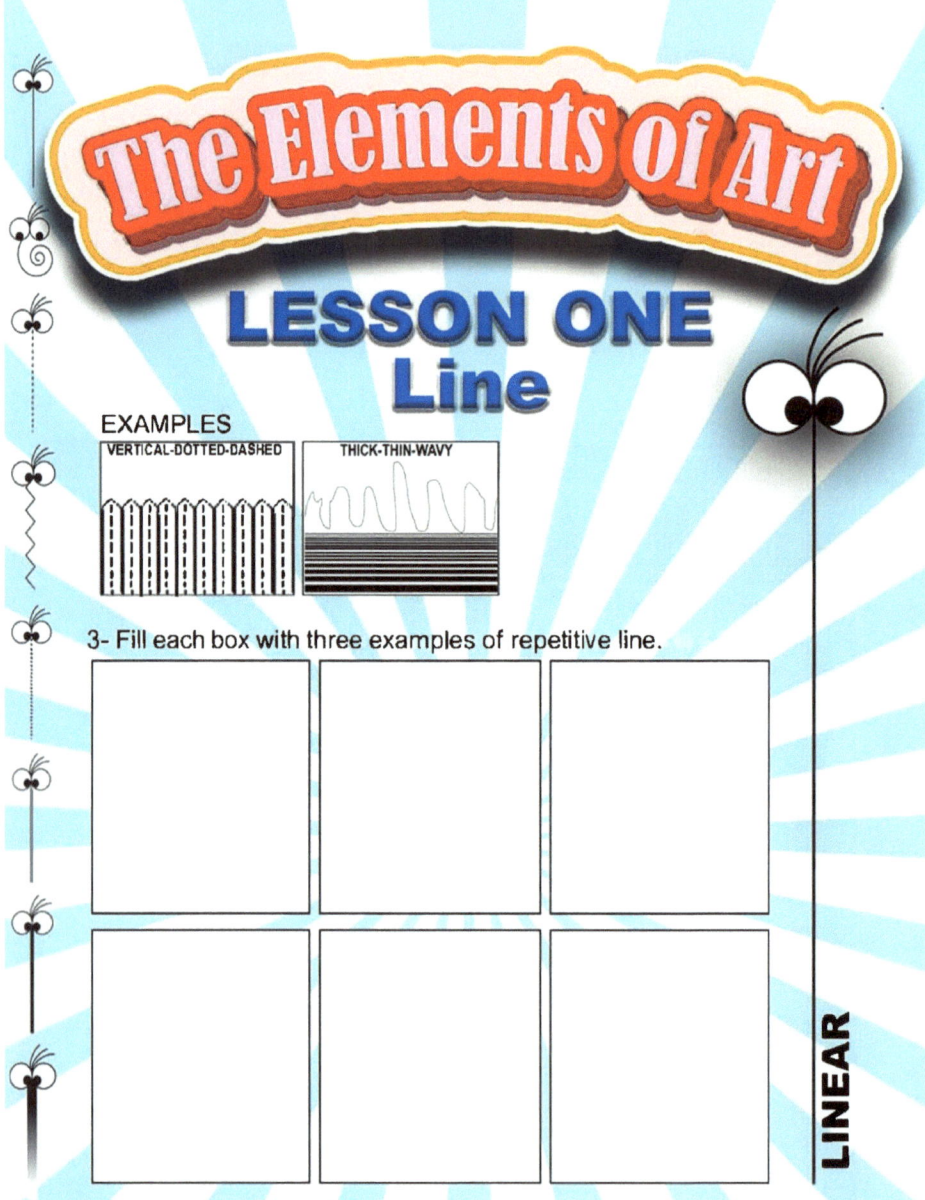

| VERTICAL-DOTTED-DASHED | THICK-THIN-WAVY |

3- Fill each box with three examples of repetitive line.

**LINEAR**

6

# The Elements of Art

## LESSON ONE
## Line

4- This picture has various examples of lines. Highlight the examples with your pencil or marker..

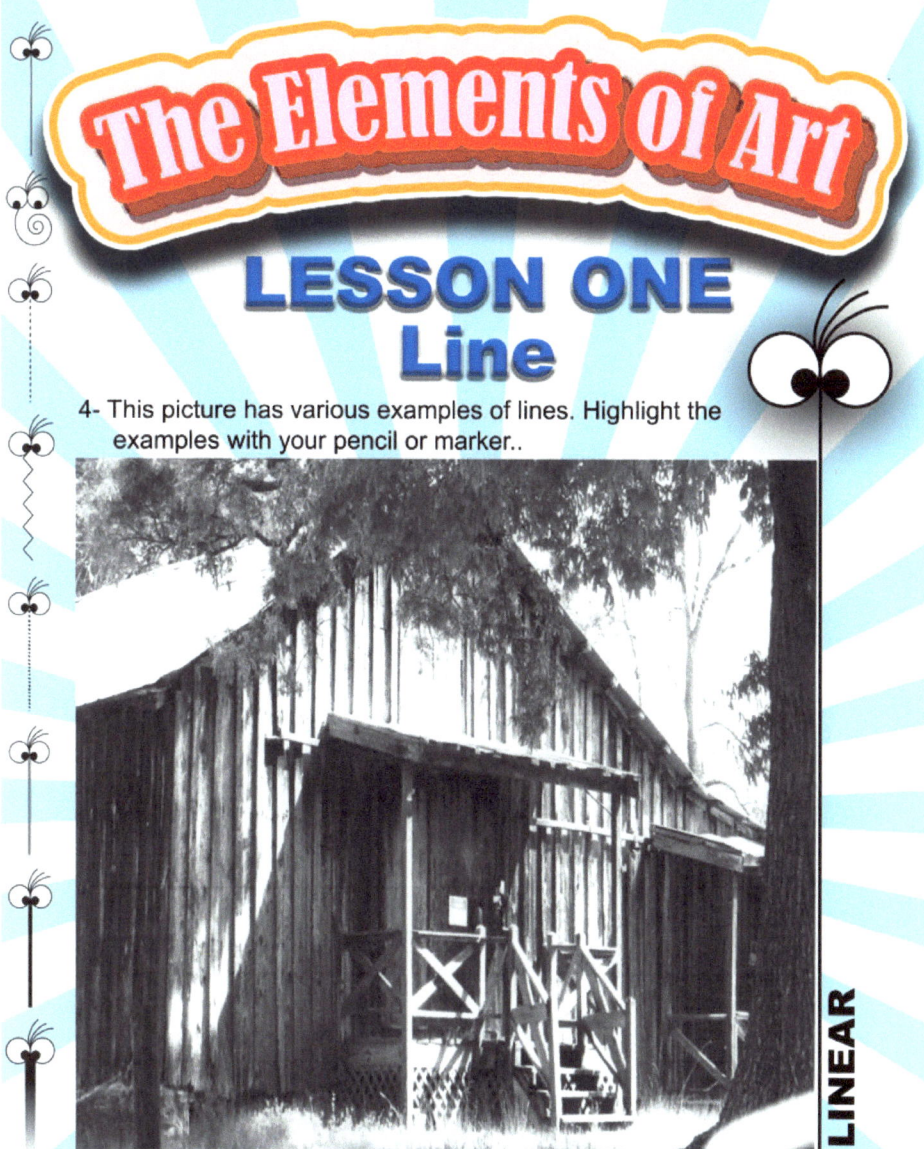

LINEAR

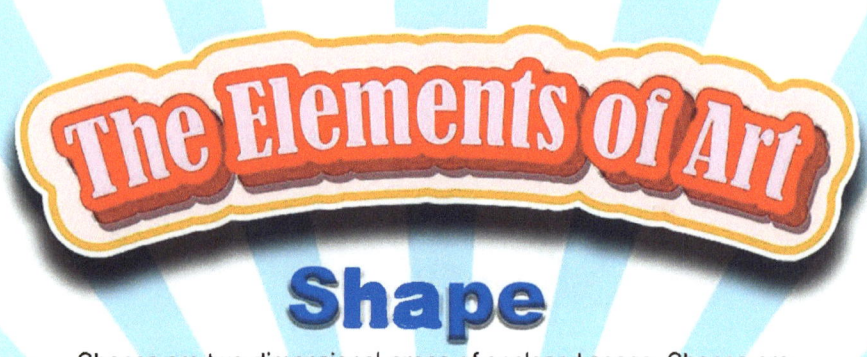

# Shape

Shapes are two-dimensional areas of enclosed space. Shapes are flat and only have height and width.

There are two groups of SHAPES:

**GEOMETRIC SHAPES:**
We can find them in The Human Made enviroment.

**ORGANIC SHAPES:**
We can find them in Nature.

| | |
|---|---|
| **SQUARE** | **ANIMALS** |
| **RECTANGLE** | **DOGS** |
| **TRIANGLE** | **PLANTS** |
| **CIRCLE** | **TREES** |
| **ELLIPSE** | **WATER** |
| **PENTAGON** | **FISH** |

# The Elements of Art

## LESSON TWO
## Geometric Shape

Supplies needed: drawing pad, pencils/markers.

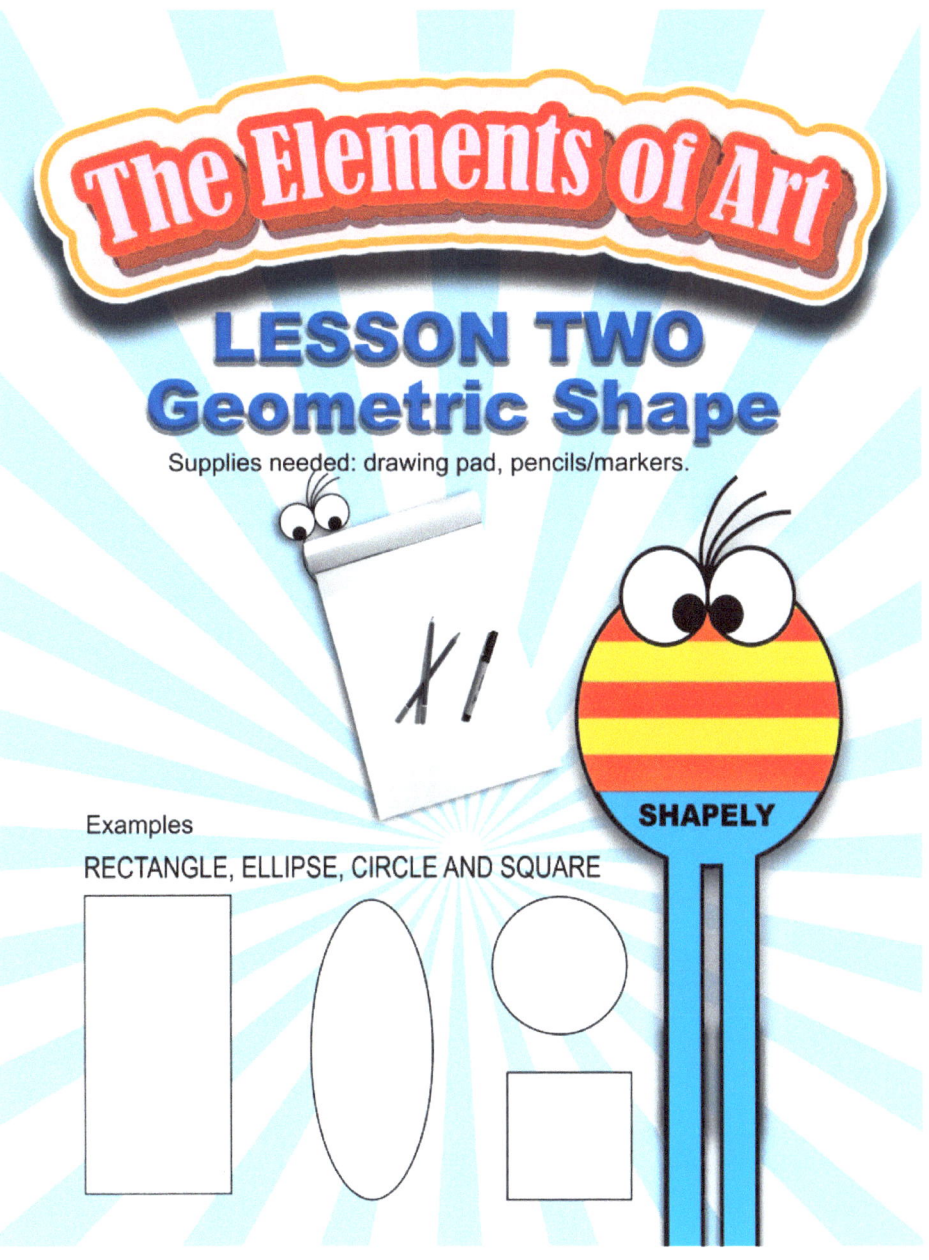

Examples

RECTANGLE, ELLIPSE, CIRCLE AND SQUARE

SHAPELY

# The Elements of Art

## LESSON TWO
## Geometric Shape

EXAMPLES

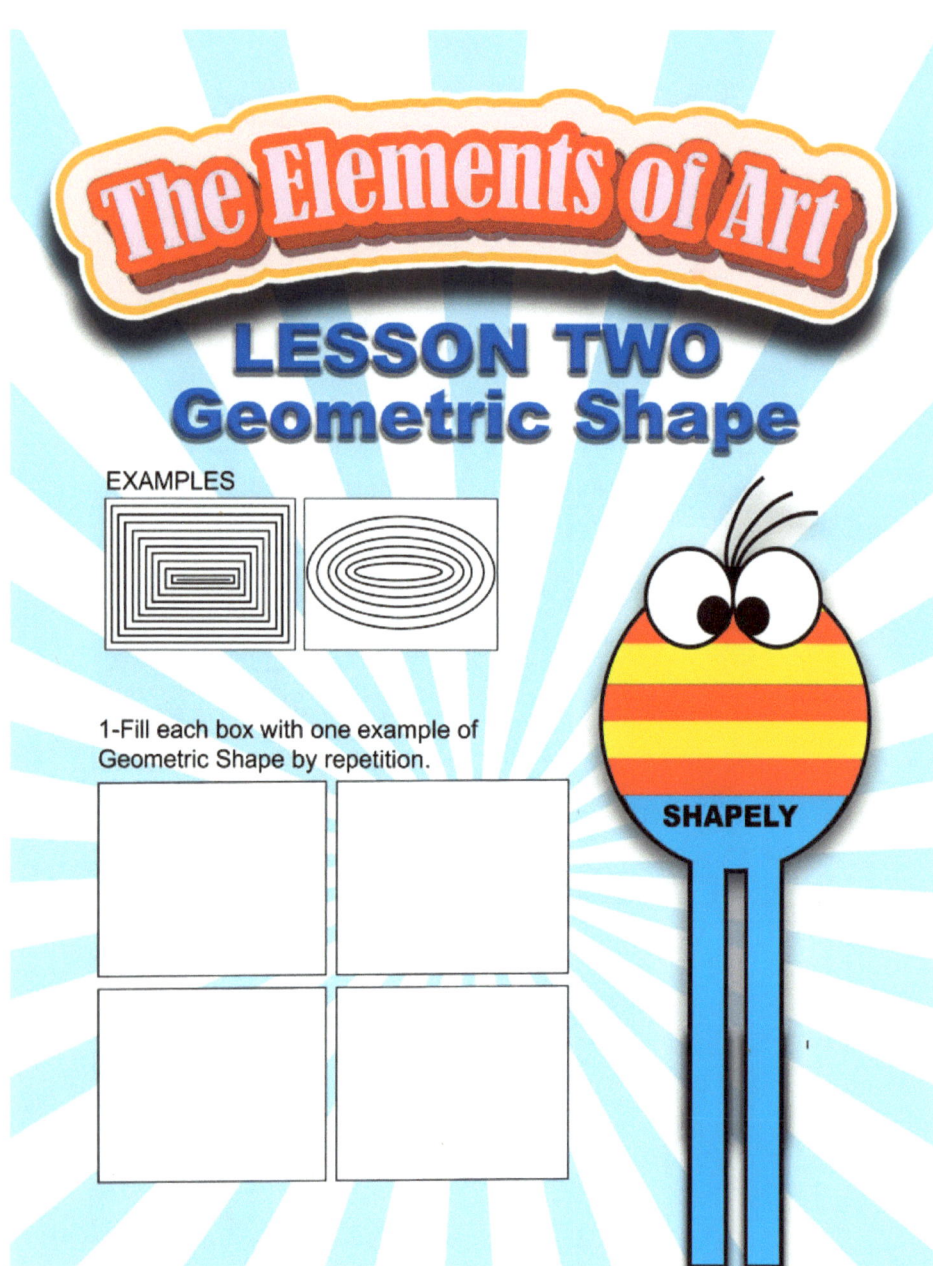

1-Fill each box with one example of Geometric Shape by repetition.

SHAPELY

# The Elements of Art

## LESSON TWO
## Geometric Shape

EXAMPLES

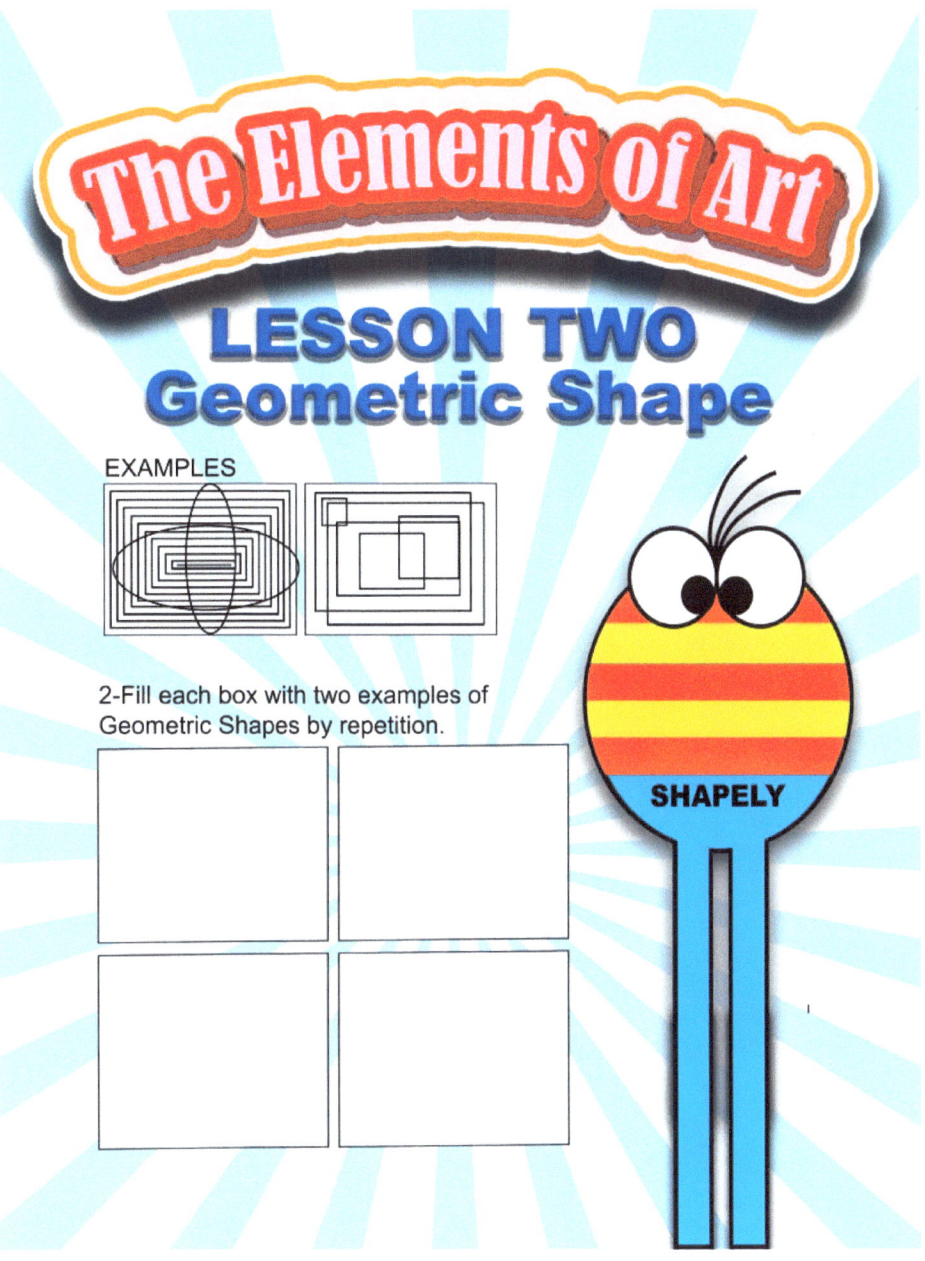

2-Fill each box with two examples of Geometric Shapes by repetition.

SHAPELY

# The Elements of Art

## LESSON TWO
## Geometric Shape

3- This picture has various examples of GEOMETRIC SHAPES. Highlight the examples with your pencil or marker.

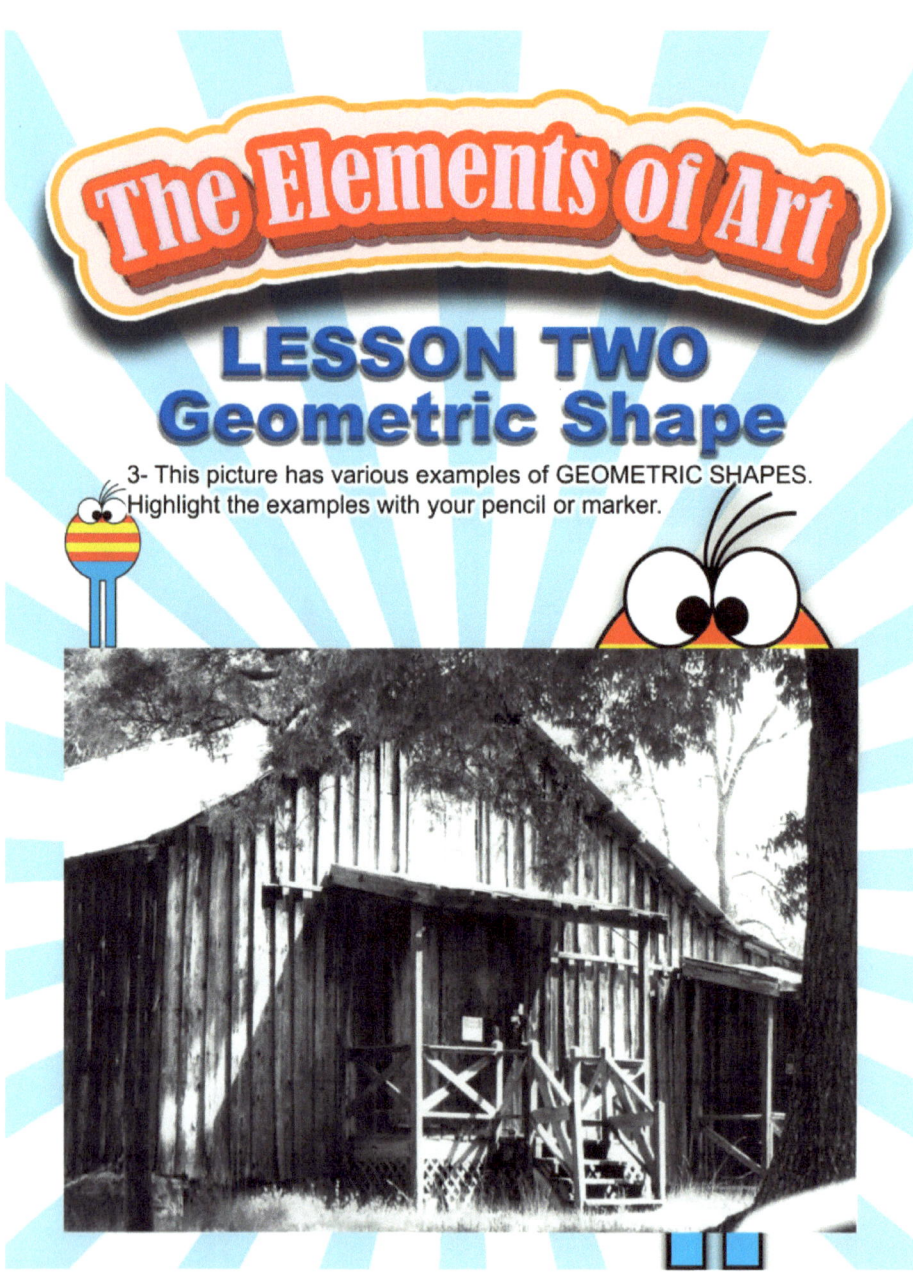

# The Elements of Art

## LESSON TWO
## Organic Shape

Supplies needed: drawing pad and pencils/markers.

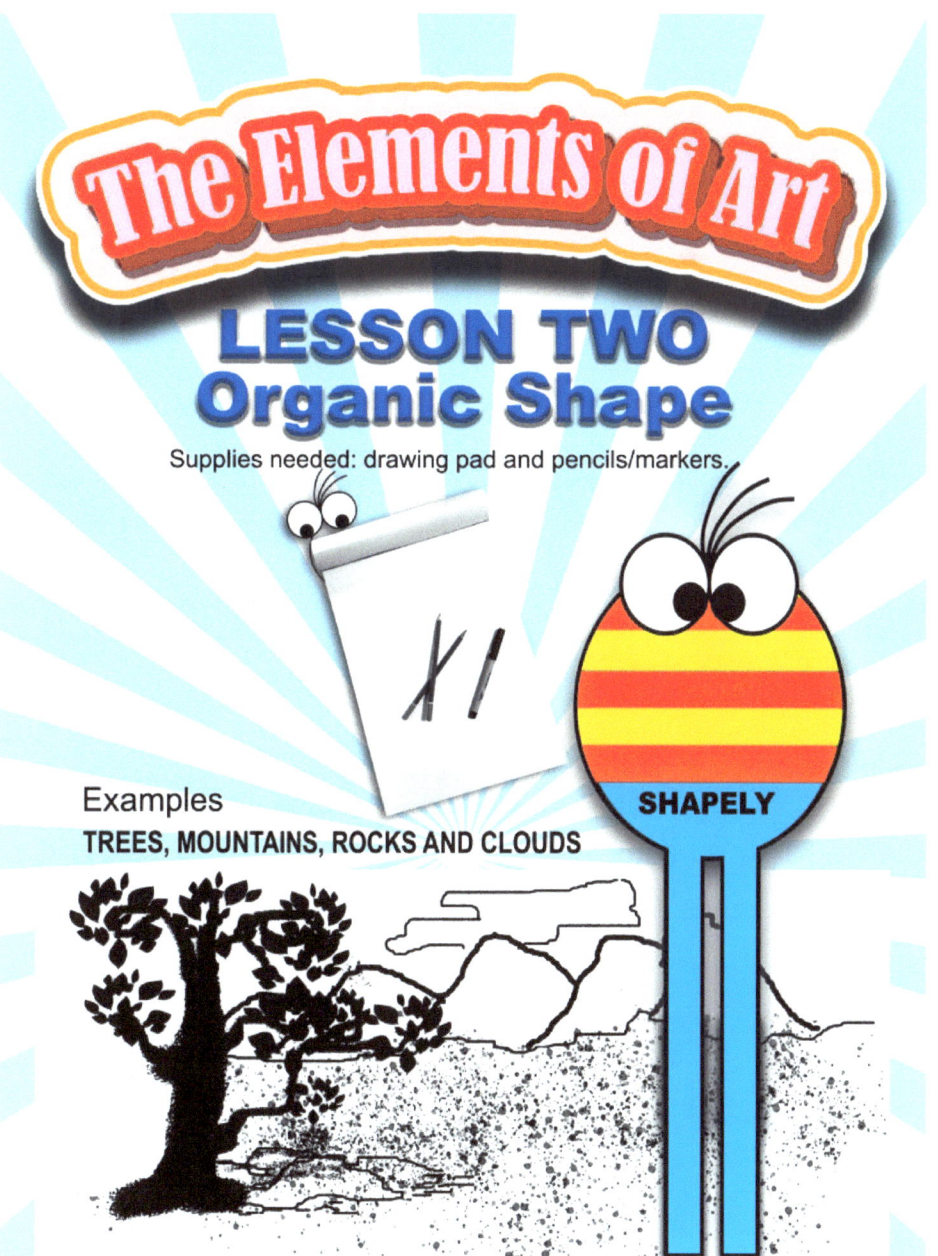

Examples

**TREES, MOUNTAINS, ROCKS AND CLOUDS**

SHAPELY

# The Elements of Art

## LESSON TWO
## Organic Shape

EXAMPLES

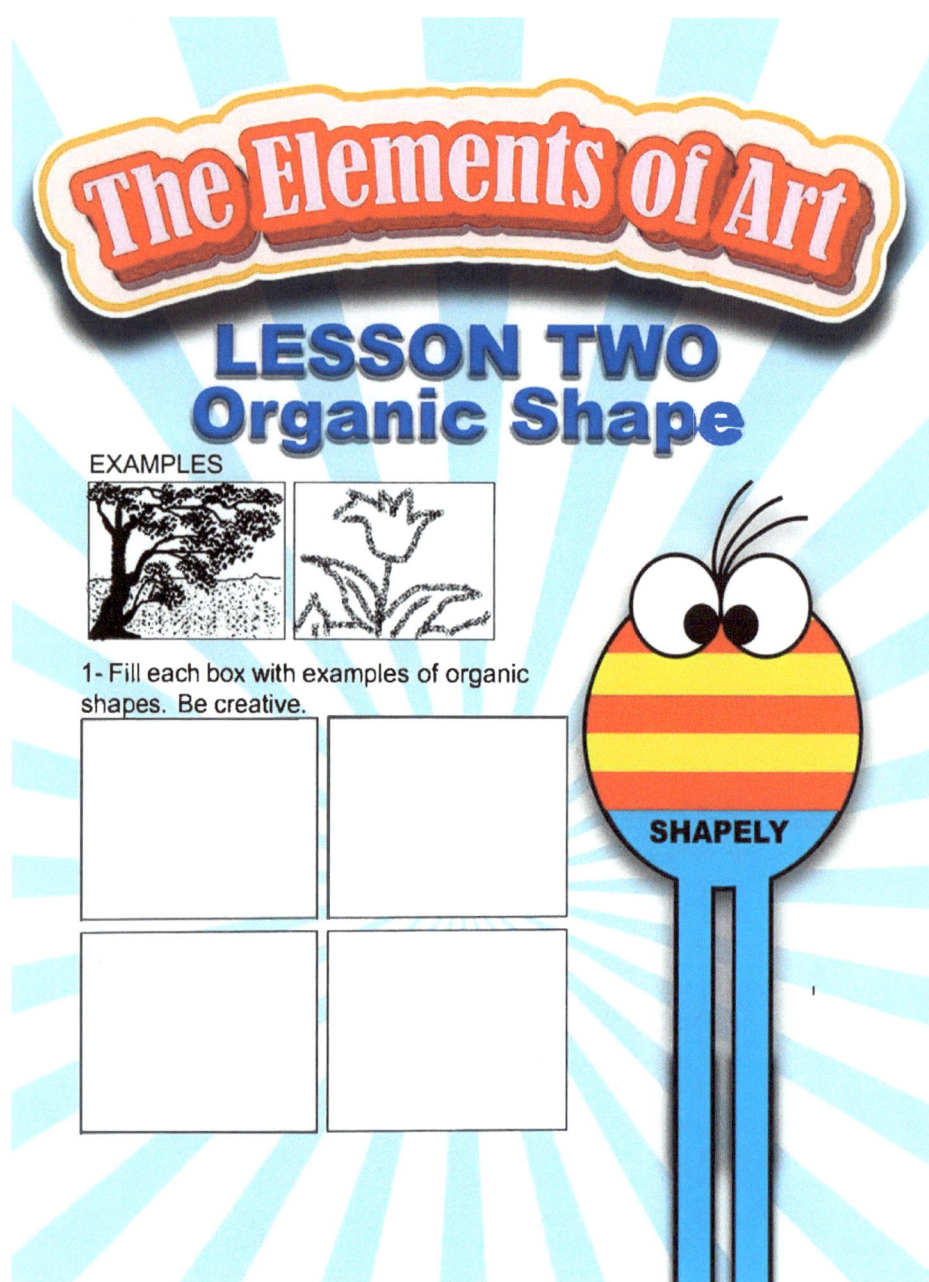

1- Fill each box with examples of organic shapes. Be creative.

SHAPELY

# The Elements of Art

## LESSON TWO
## Organic Shape

2- This picture has various examples of organic shapes. Outline the examples with your marker.

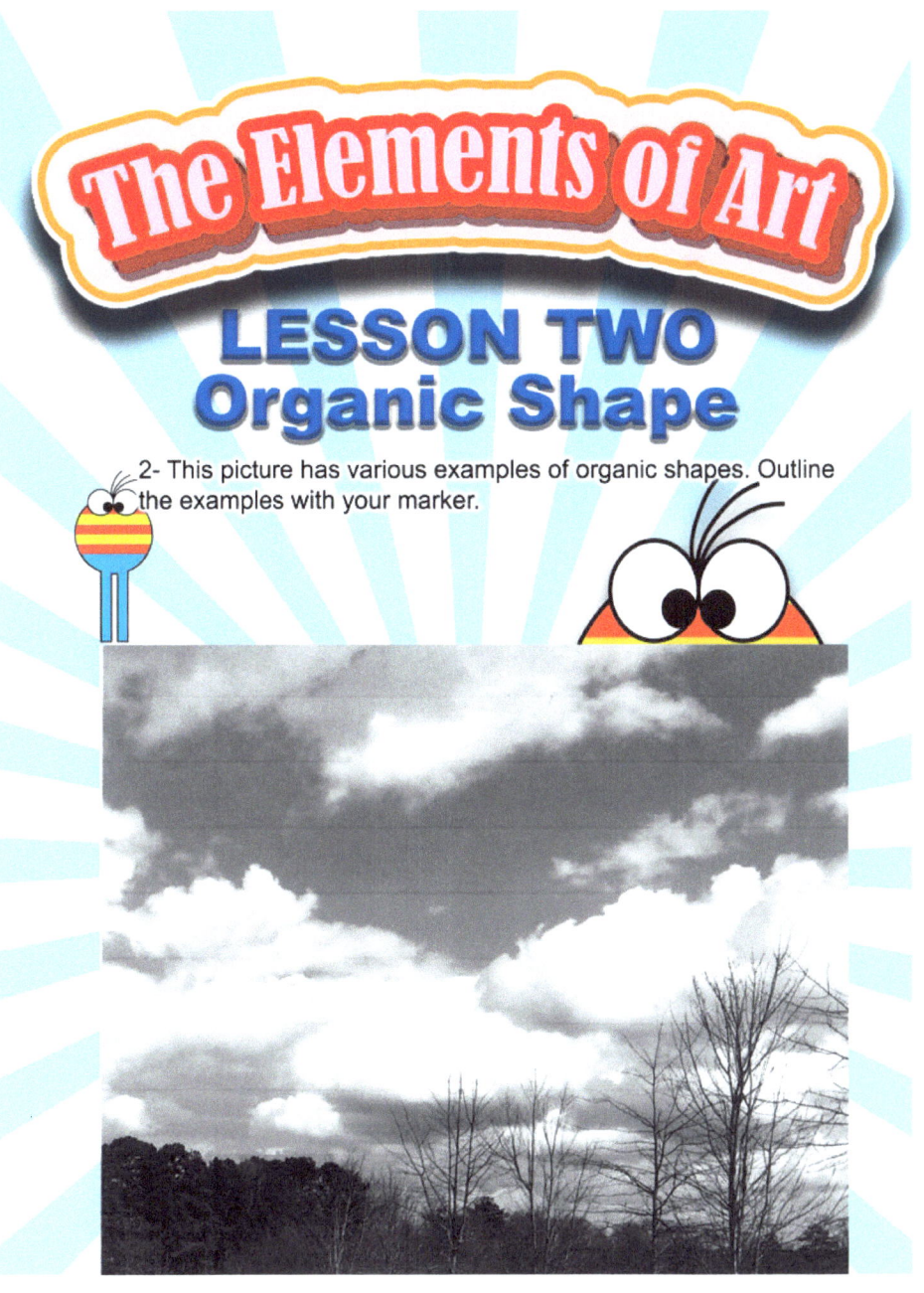

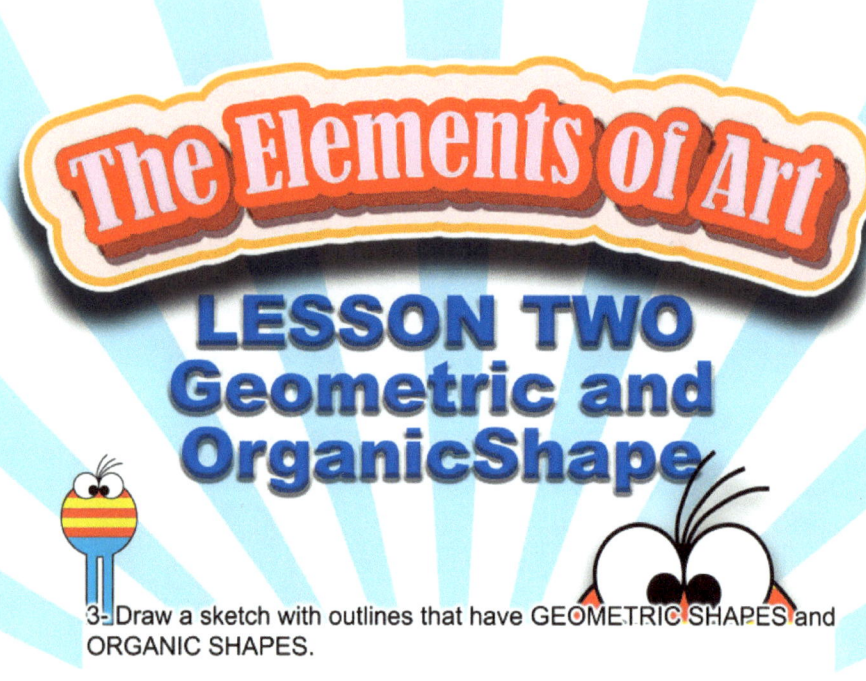

# The Elements of Art

## LESSON TWO
## Geometric and OrganicShape

3- Draw a sketch with outlines that have GEOMETRIC SHAPES and ORGANIC SHAPES.

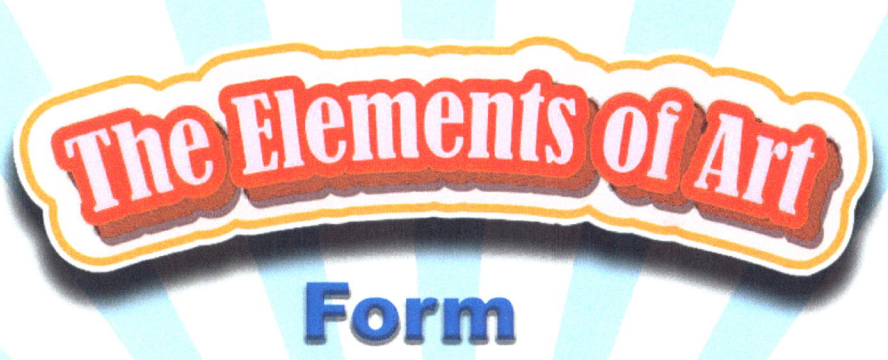

# Form

Form is an element of art that is three-dimensional.
Form has height, width and depth like a sculpture.

GEOMETRIC FORM:
We can find them in The Human Made
Enviroment.

ORGANIC FORM:
We can find them in NATURE.

**CUBE**
**SPHERE**
**CYLINDER**
**PYRAMID**
**CONE**

**CATS**
**DOGS**
**PLANTS**
**FLOWERS**
**FISH**

# The Elements of Art

## LESSON THREE
## Geometric Form

Supplies needed: drawing pad, pencils or markers.

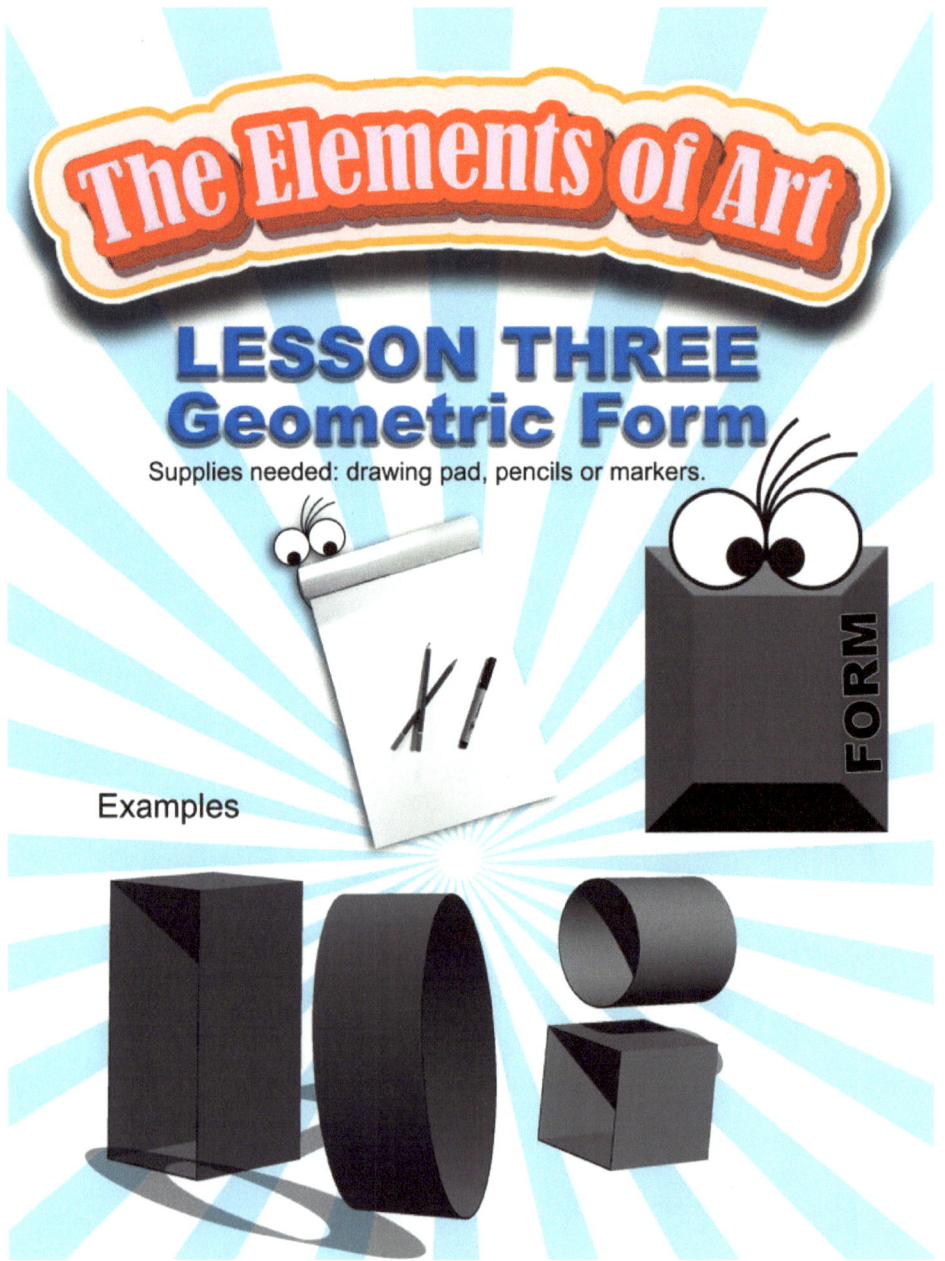

Examples

FORM

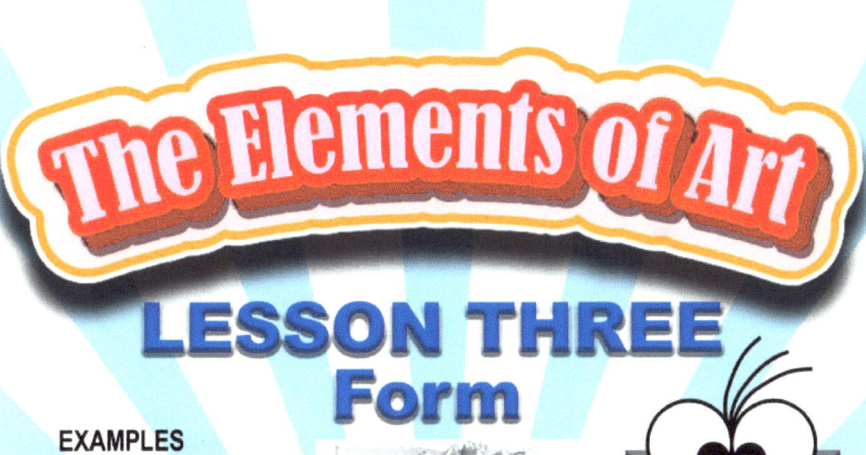

# LESSON THREE
## Form

**EXAMPLES**

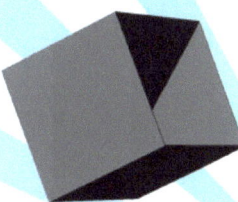

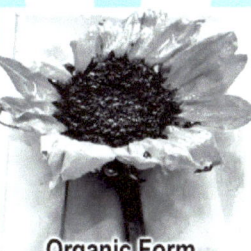

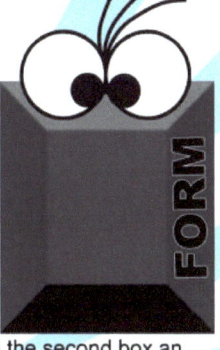

**Geometric Form**          **Organic Form**

1- Draw in the first box an example of geometric form and in the second box an example of organic form using lines and shapes to complete the form artwork. BE CREATIVE.

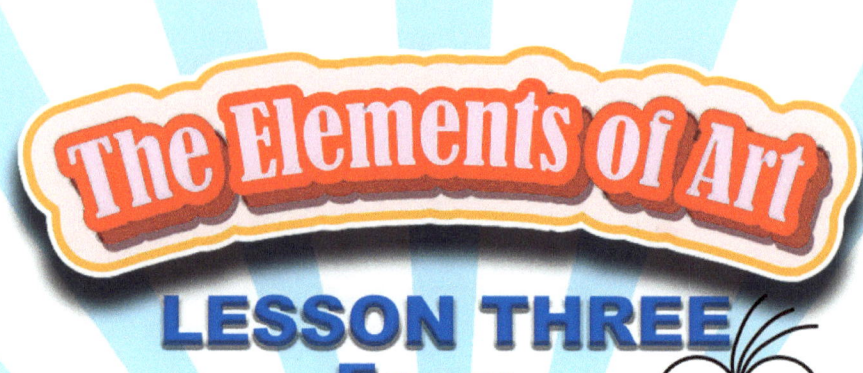

# The Elements of Art

## LESSON THREE
## Form

2- Look around the room and find a 3D form and use lines and shapes to draw the 3D form inside the white box below. BE CREATIVE.

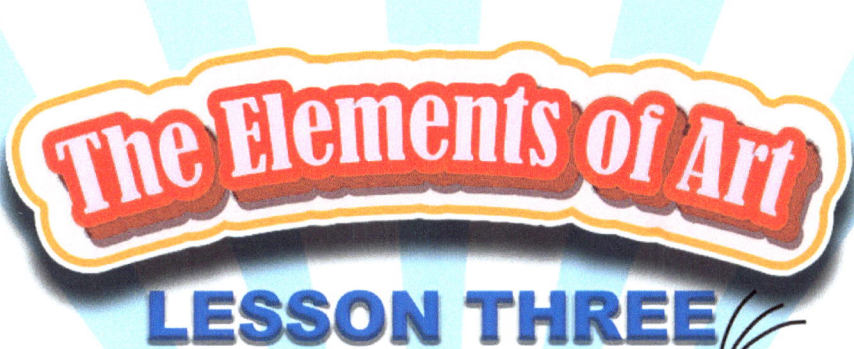

# LESSON THREE
## Form

3- Take one of your 3D shoe and use lines and shapes to draw the 3D shoe form inside the white box below. BE CREATIVE.

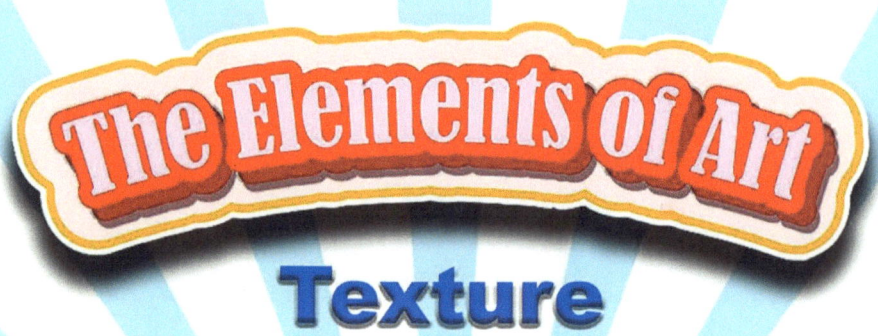

# Texture

An element of art that is used to describe how something feels or looks.
There are many Actual and Visual textures.

## VISUAL TEXTURES:

They are two-dimensional and are perceived by the eye that makes it seem like the texture. They look like texture but they are flat.

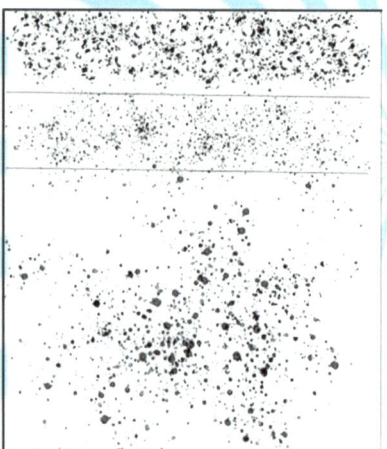

## ACTUAL TEXTURES:

There are 3D visible and tactile textures. You can see and feel the texture rising above the surface. They look like texture and they feel like texture.

**GRAINY**

**ROUGH**

**FLUFFY**

**BUMPY**

**SOFT**

**HARD**

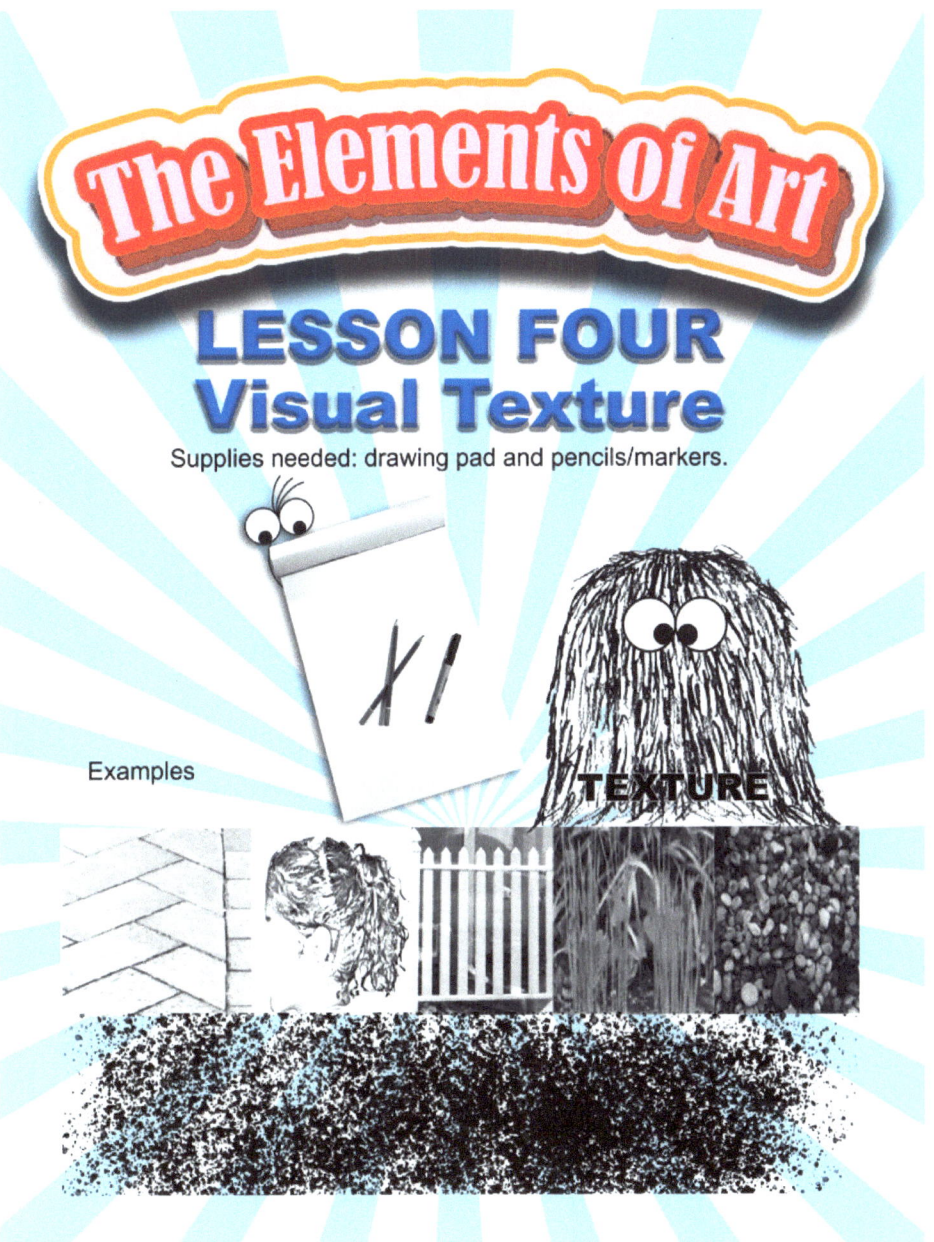

# The Elements of Art

## LESSON FOUR
## Visual Texture

Supplies needed: drawing pad and pencils/markers.

Examples

TEXTURE

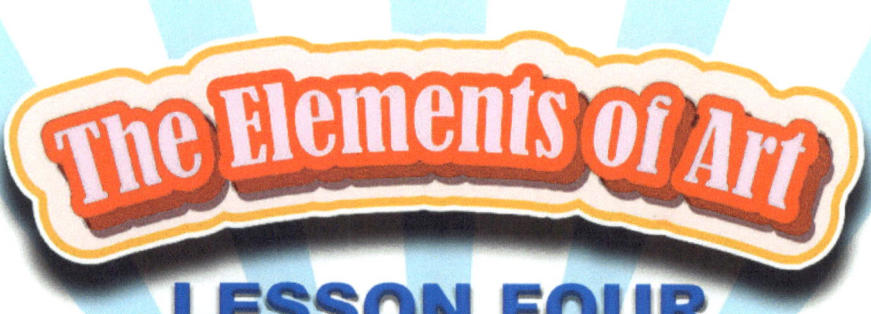

# LESSON FOUR
# Visual Texture

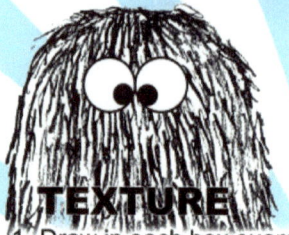

## TEXTURE

1- Draw in each box examples of visual textures using lines and shapes to complete the artwork. BE CREATIVE.

# The Elements of Art

## LESSON FOUR
### Texture

2- Make a copy of a picture in a magazine page in black and white. The picture should have diferent visual textures. using a marker, trace the lines that create the visual texture. BE CREATIVE.

### EXAMPLE

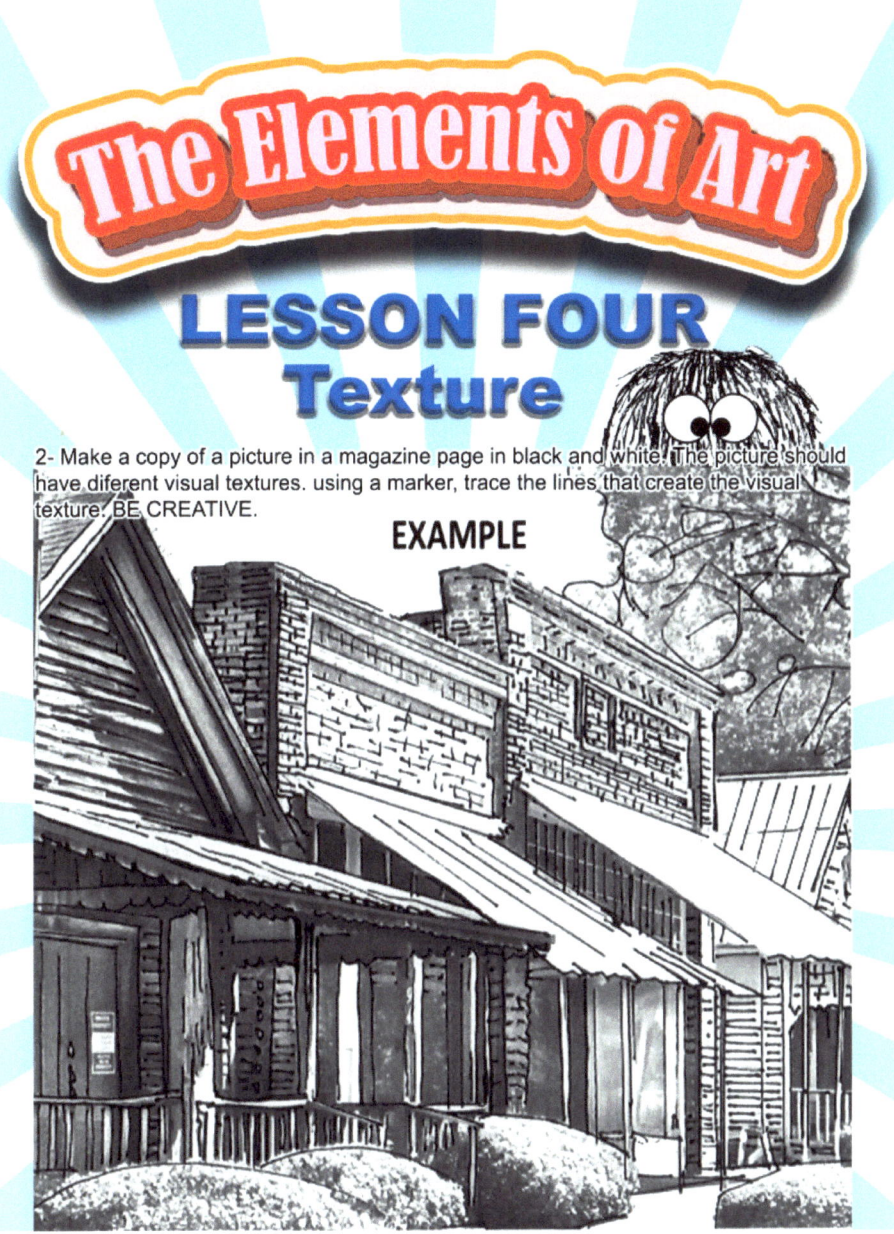

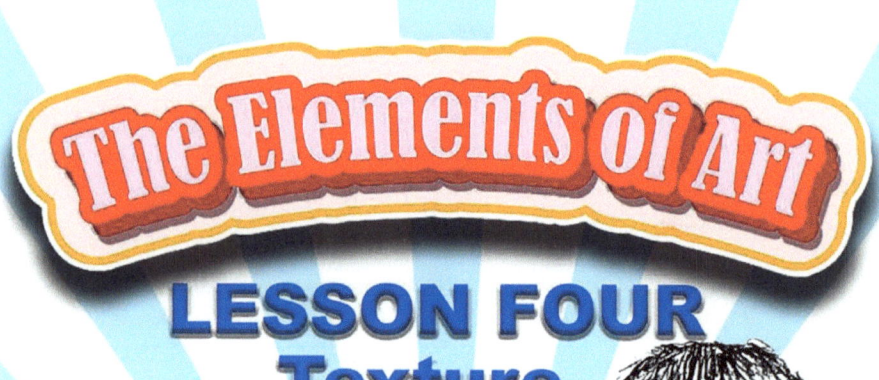

# The Elements of Art

## LESSON FOUR
## Texture

3- Go outside and find different items in nature with different types of texture Glue them on a paper and label them with the name of the type of texture: smooth, soft, fuzzy, etc. BE CREATIVE.

# The Elements of Art

# LESSON FIVE
# Color

**COLOR** is produced when the light striking an object is reflected back to the eye. Color is made up of three properties:

**1-Hue:** name of color.
- **PRIMARY COLORS:** red, blue and yellow.
- **SECONDARY COLORS:** green, orange and violet.
- **INTERMEDIATE COLORS:** red-orange, yellow-orange, yellow-green, blue-green, blue-violet and red-violet

**2-Value:** lightness and darkness of a color.

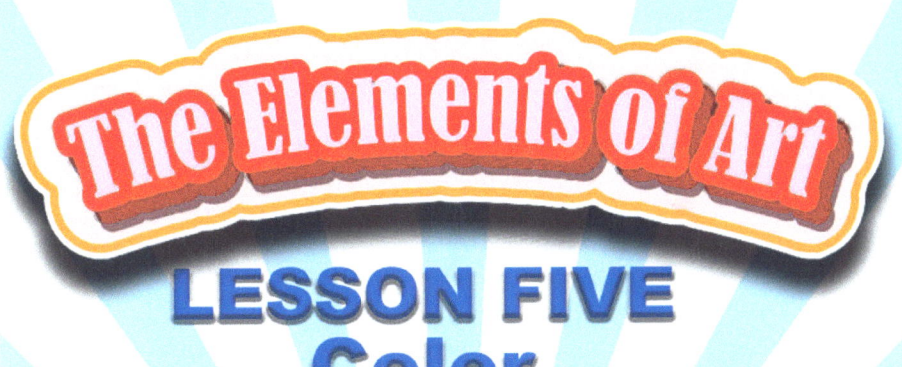

**3-Intensity:** quality, brightness and purity of a color.

| high intensity=<br>color is strong and bright | low intensity=<br>color is faint and dull). |
|---|---|

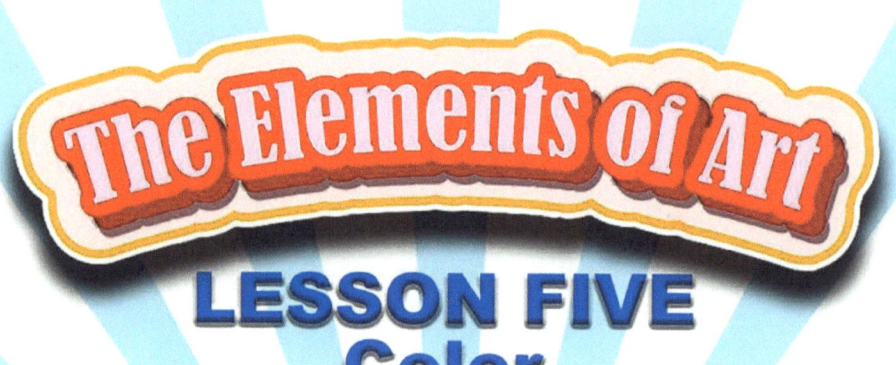

# LESSON FIVE
## Color

**Supplies needed:** drawing pad, primary colors paint, q-tips, plastic plates, ruler, color pencils.

Using a page from the drawing pad, draw 2 intersecting triangles. Label the primary colors using the pencils and drop a primary color with the Q-tips.

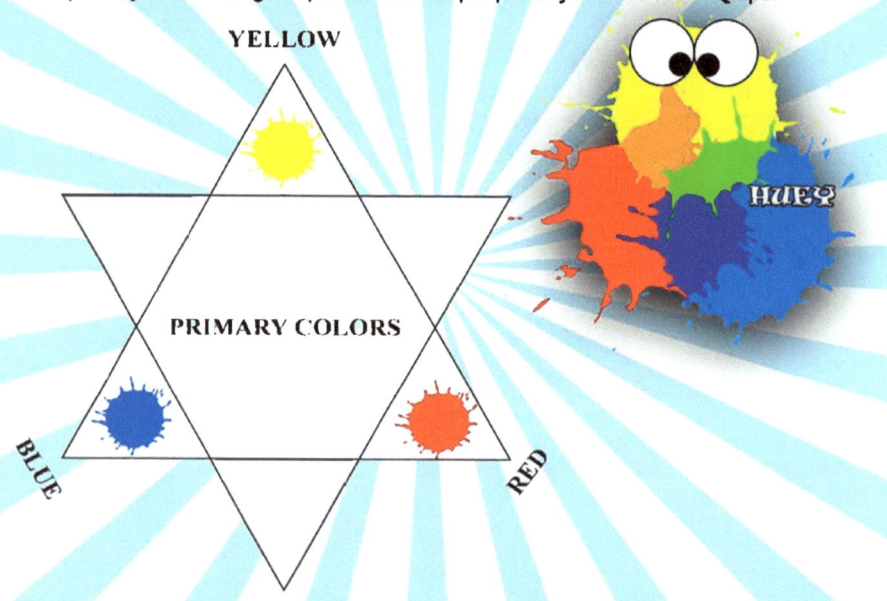

YELLOW

PRIMARY COLORS

BLUE

RED

HUEY

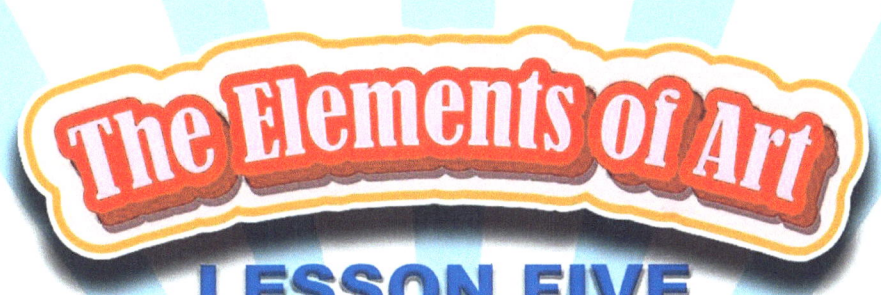

# LESSON FIVE
## Color

**Supplies needed: drawing pad, primary colors paint, q-tips, plastic plates, ruler, color pencils.**

Using a page from the drawing pad, draw 2 intersecting triangles. Label the primary and secondary colors with the color pencils. Use a Q-tip to place a drop of each of the colors. See example below.

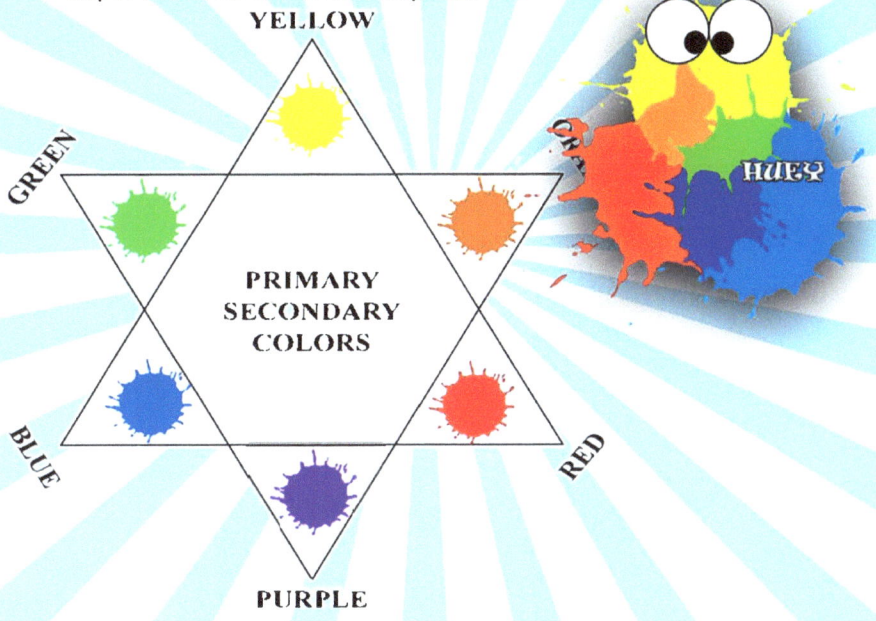

29

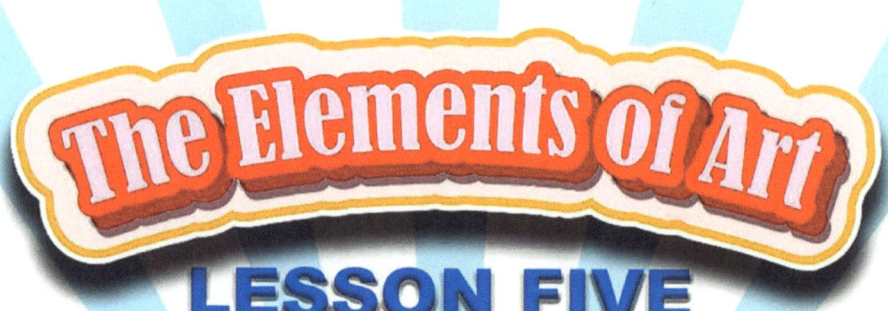

# LESSON FIVE
## Color

**Supplies needed: drawing pad, primary colors paint, q-tips, plastic plates, ruler, color pencils.**

Using a page from the drawing pad, draw **2** intersecting triangles. Label the primary, secondary and intermediate colors with the color pencils. Use a Q-tip to place a drop of each of the colors. See example below.

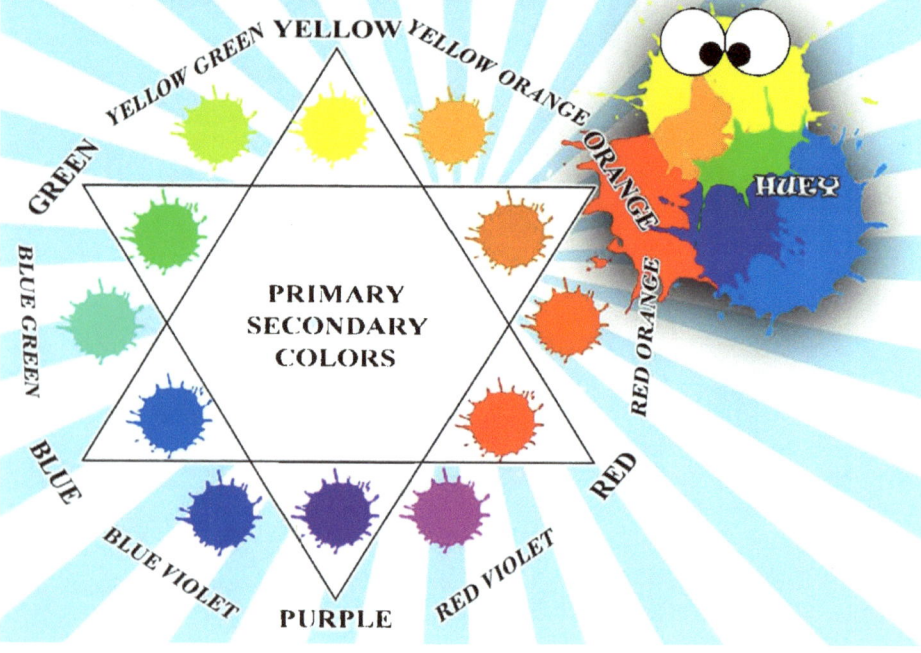

30

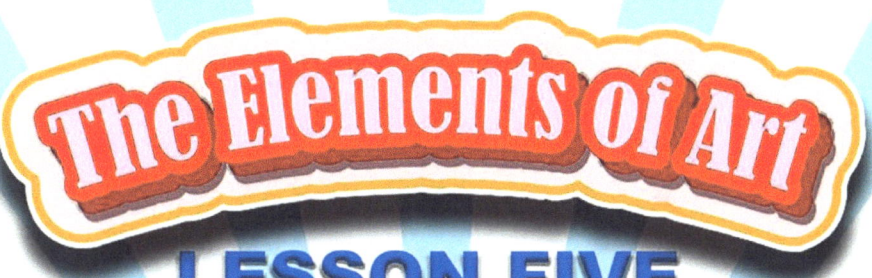

# The Elements of Art

## LESSON FIVE
## Color

**Supplies needed:** drawing pad, red, orange and yellow paint, q-tips, plastic plates, and color pencils.

These are colors that evoke warmth because they remind us of things like the sun or fire. These colors are called **WARM COLORS**. Using all warm colors show the **VALUE** (the darkness or lightness of each color) inside the box.

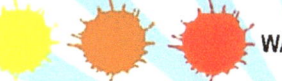 **WARM COLORS**

**EXAMPLE**

HUEY

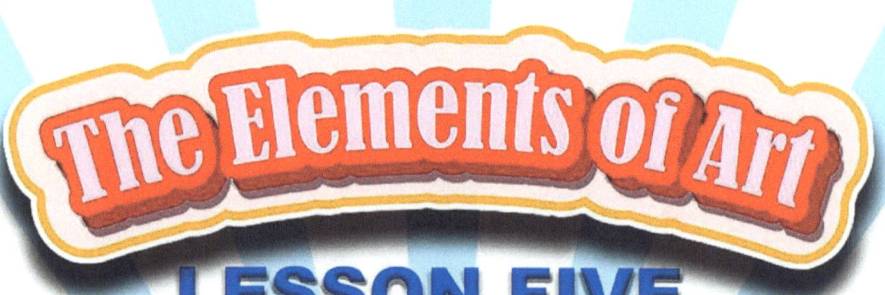

## LESSON FIVE
## Color

Supplies needed: drawing pad, red, orange and yellow paint, q-tips, plastic plates, and color pencils.

There are colors that evoke a cool feeling because they remind us of things like water or grass. These colors are called COOL COLORS. Using all cool colors show the VALUE (darkness or lightness of each color) inside the box.

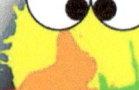

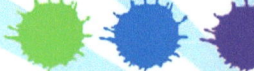 COOL COLORS

**EXAMPLE**

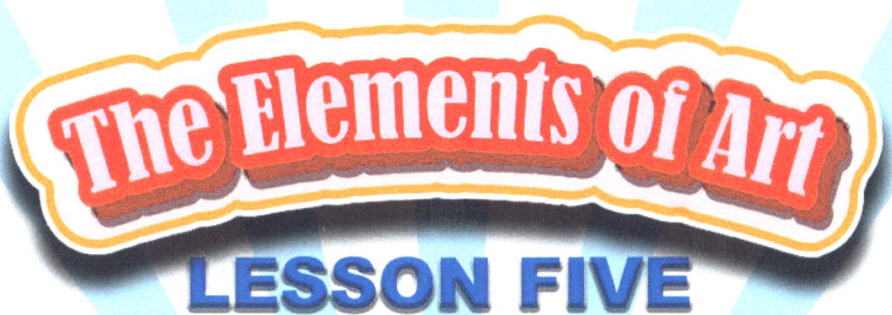

# LESSON FIVE
## Color

COMPLEMENTARY COLORS are also known as the opposite colors, because they are in opposite locations of the color wheel. When the complementary colors are placed next to each other, they create the strongest contrast for those two color's sides of the color wheel.

EXAMPLE

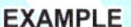

Using the color wheel below, show all the diferent combinations of complementary colors using color paint.

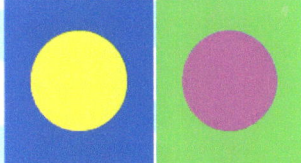

**COLOR WHEEL**

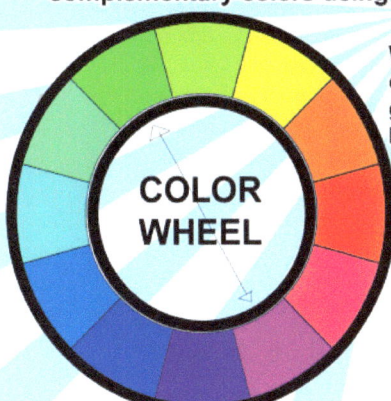

When we mix or combine complementary colors, they lose the hue by producing a grayscale color like white or black. Mix each two color combination of complementary colors to prove it.

EXAMPLE: MIX

+ ● = ?

33

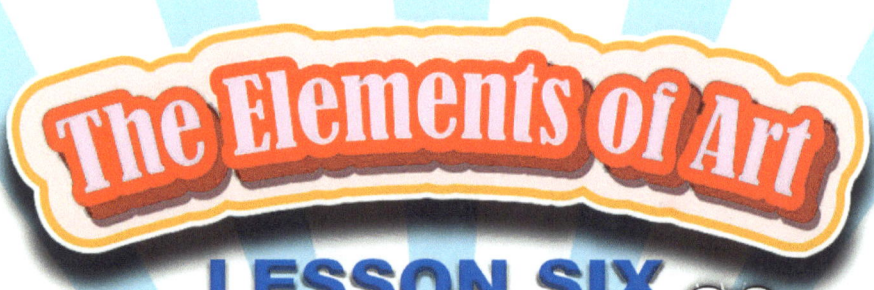

# LESSON SIX
## Value

**VALUE**

The lightness or darkness of a color. White is the lightest value and black is the darkest. The value halfway between white and black is called middle gray.

Tints are lighter versions of the color that are made by mixing a color with white and shades are darker versions of the color that are made by mixing a color with black. A tone is produced either by mixing a color with grey, or by both tinting and shading.

## TINT     TONE     SHADE

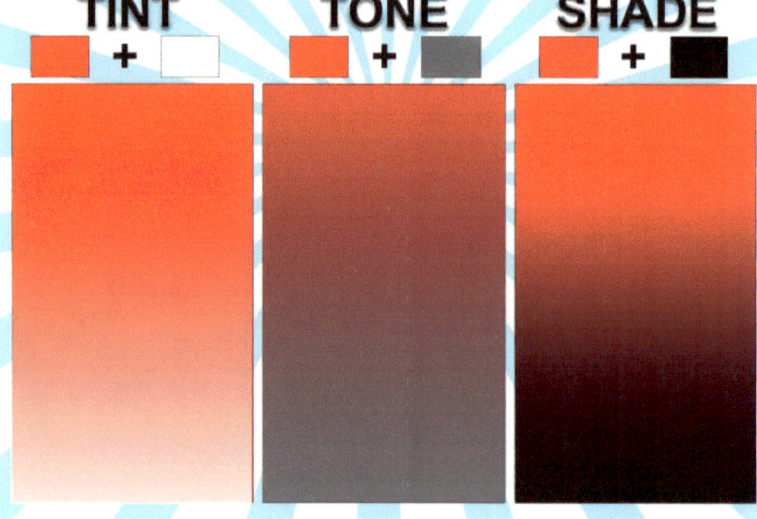

# The Elements of Art

## LESSON SIX
## Value

Using the primary colors (RED BLUE AND YELLOW) add 1, 2, 3, 4 drops of white to each primary color to get the different range of tints.

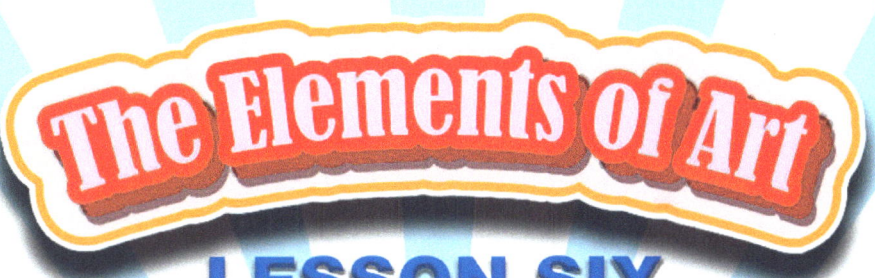

**TINT**

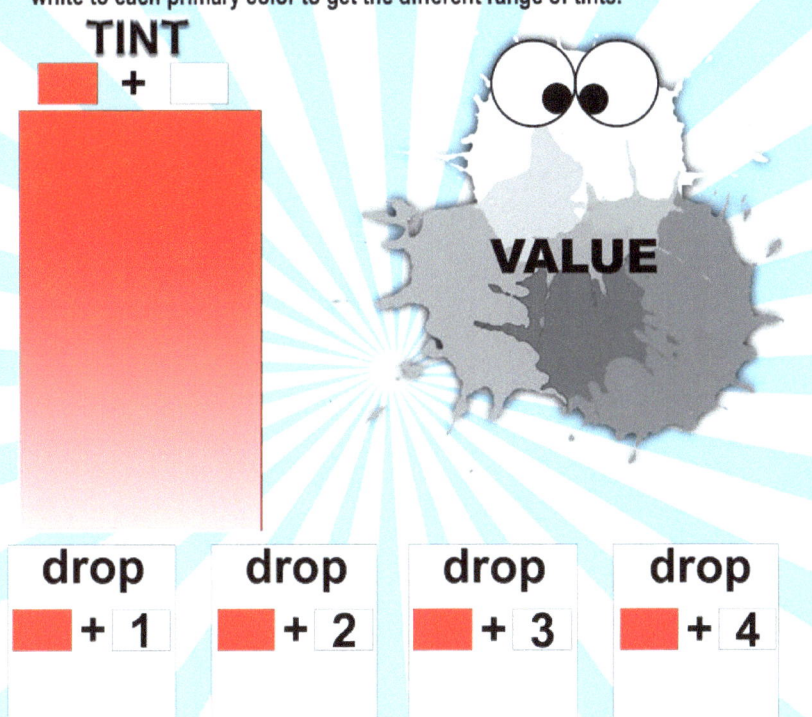

**VALUE**

| drop | drop | drop | drop |
|------|------|------|------|
| + 1 | + 2 | + 3 | + 4 |

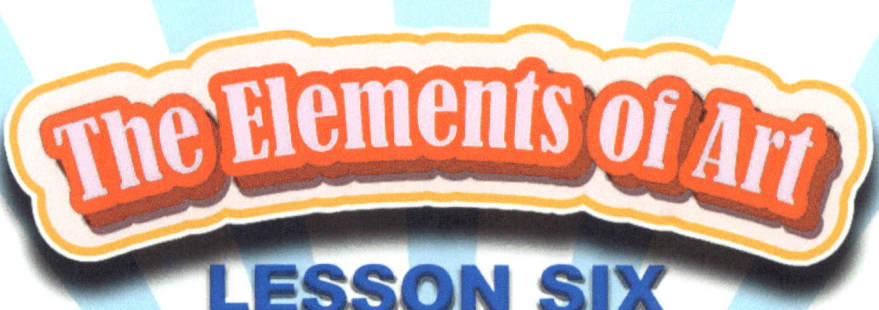

# LESSON SIX
## Value

Using the secondary colors (green, orange and violet) add 1, 2, 3, 4 drops of white to each secondary color to get the different color range of tints.

**TINT** + 

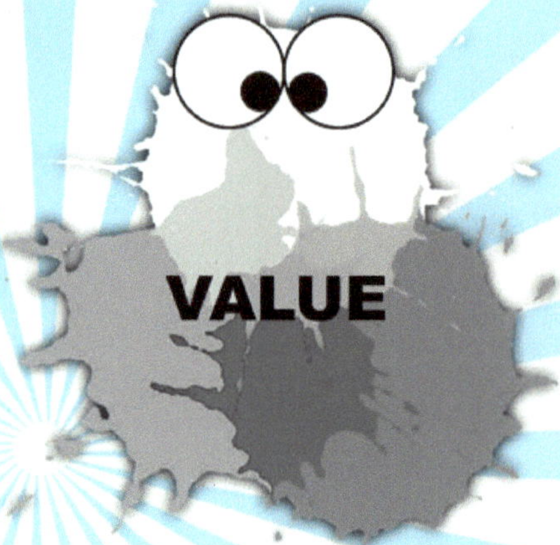

**VALUE**

| drop + 1 | drop + 2 | drop + 3 | drop + 4 |

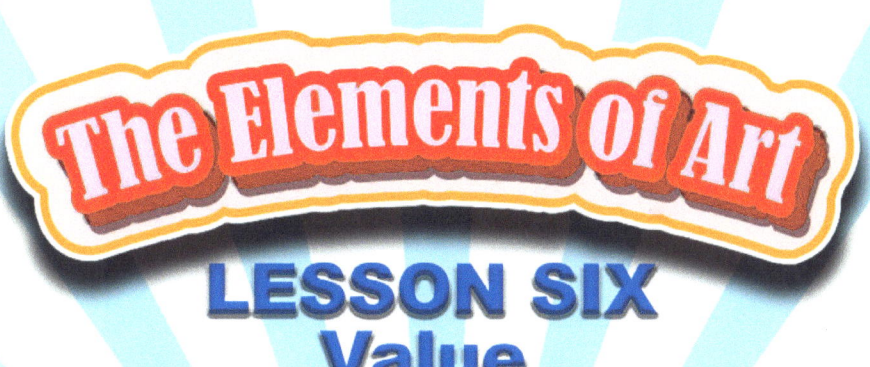

# LESSON SIX
## Value

**Using the intermediate colors add 1, 2, 3, 4 drops of white to each intermediate color to get the different color range of tints.**

### TINT

+

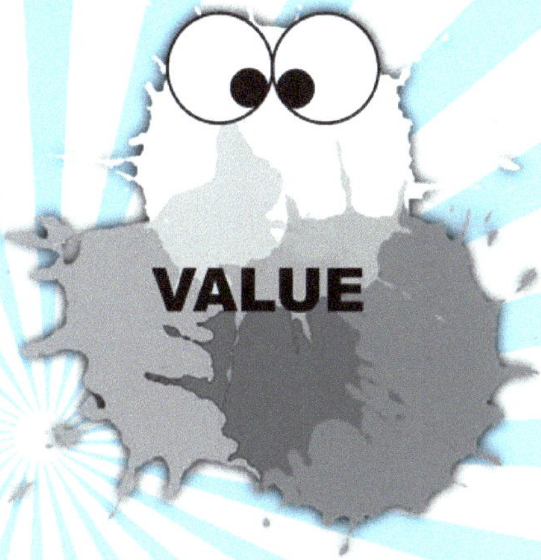

### VALUE

| drop | drop | drop | drop |
|------|------|------|------|
| + 1 | + 2 | + 3 | + 4 |

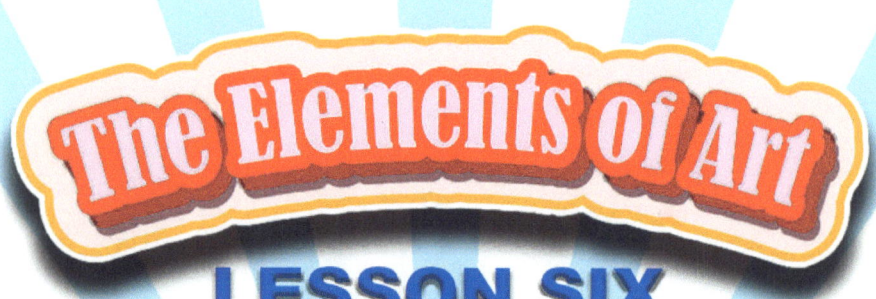

# LESSON SIX
## Value

Using the primary colors (RED-BLUE AND YELLOW) add 1, 2, 3, 4 drops of grey to each primary color to get the different range of tones.

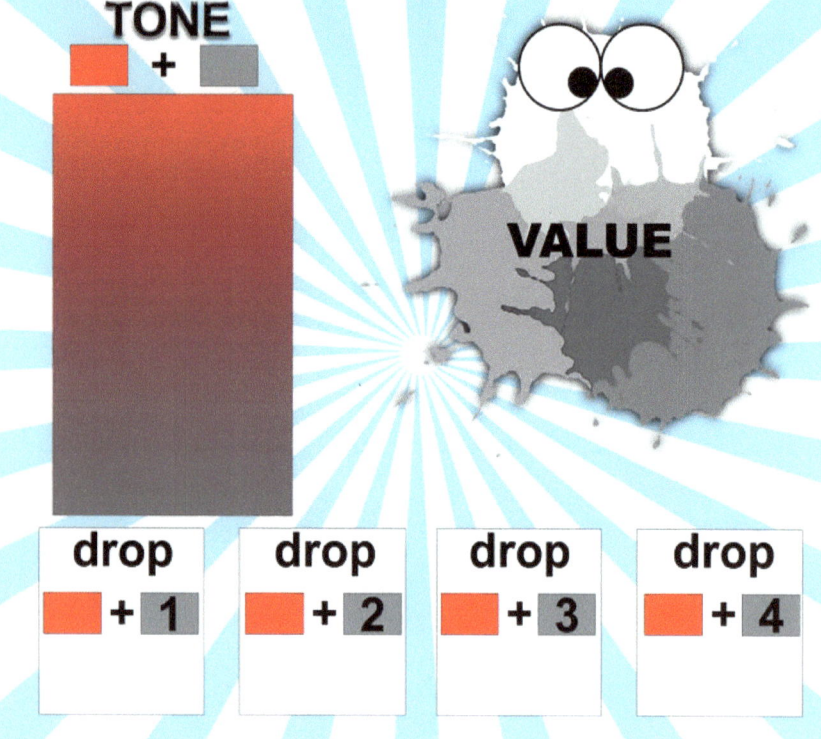

**TONE**

**VALUE**

| drop | drop | drop | drop |
|------|------|------|------|
| + 1 | + 2 | + 3 | + 4 |

# The Elements of Art

## LESSON SIX
## Value

Using the secondary colors (green, orange and violet) add 1, 2, 3, 4 drops of grey to each secondary color to get the different color range of tones.

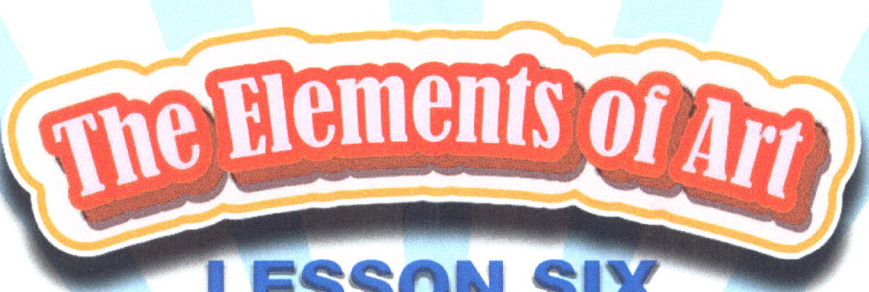

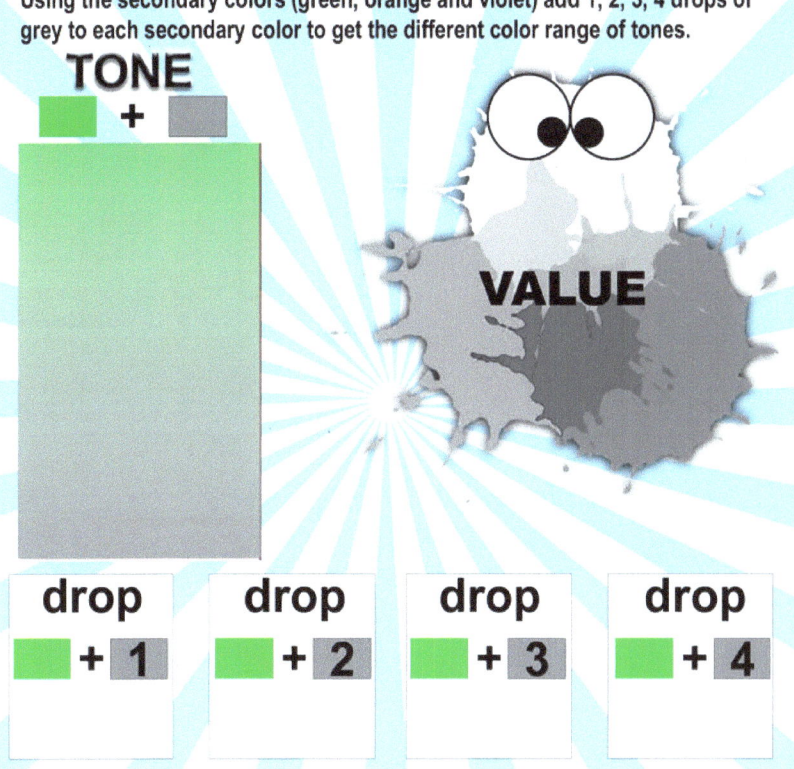

TONE

VALUE

| drop | drop | drop | drop |
|------|------|------|------|
| + 1 | + 2 | + 3 | + 4 |

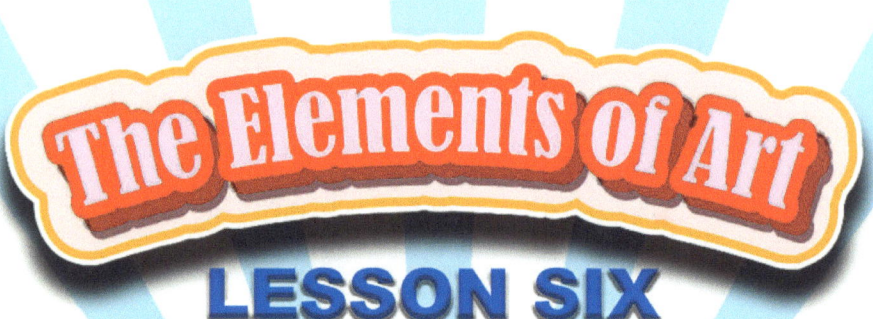

# The Elements of Art

## LESSON SIX
## Value

Using the intermediate colors add 1, 2, 3, 4 drops of GREY to each intermediate color to get the different color range of tones.

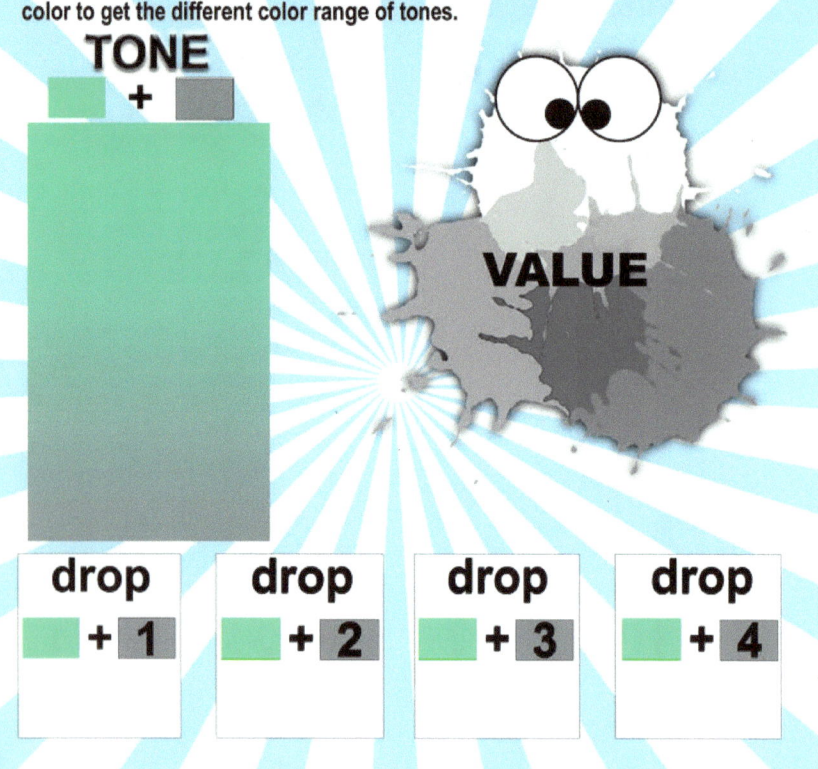

TONE
+

VALUE

drop + 1    drop + 2    drop + 3    drop + 4

# The Elements of Art

## LESSON SIX
## Value

Using the secondary colors add 1, 2, 3, 4 drops of black to each secondary color to get the different ranges of shades.

### SHADE

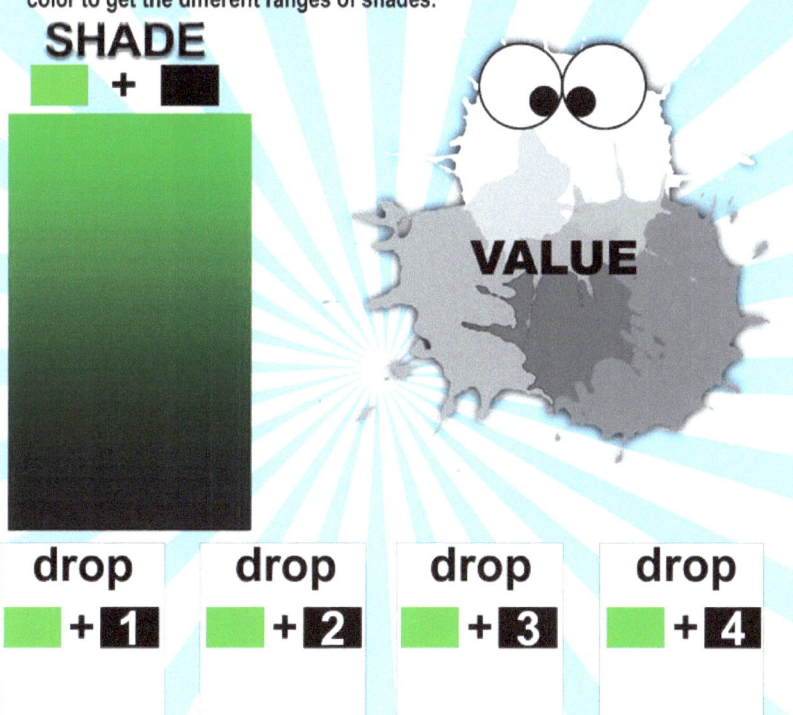

VALUE

| drop | drop | drop | drop |
|------|------|------|------|
| + 1 | + 2 | + 3 | + 4 |

# The Elements of Art

## LESSON SIX
## Value

Using the primary colors (RED BLUE AND YELLOW) add 1, 2, 3, 4 drops of black to each primary color to get the different ranges of shades.

### SHADE

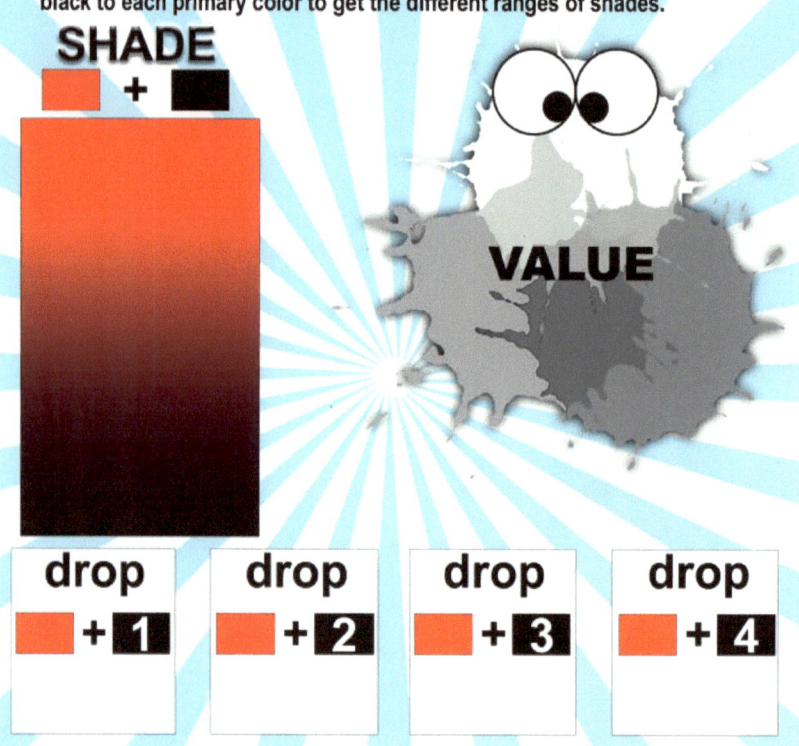

**VALUE**

| drop | drop | drop | drop |
|------|------|------|------|
| + 1 | + 2 | + 3 | + 4 |

# The Elements of Art

## LESSON SIX
## Value

Using the intermediate colors add 1, 2, 3, 4 drops of BLACK to each intermediate color to get the different color range of SHADES.

### SHADE

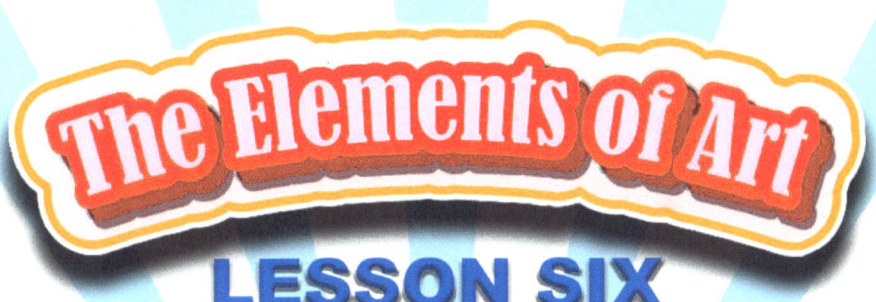

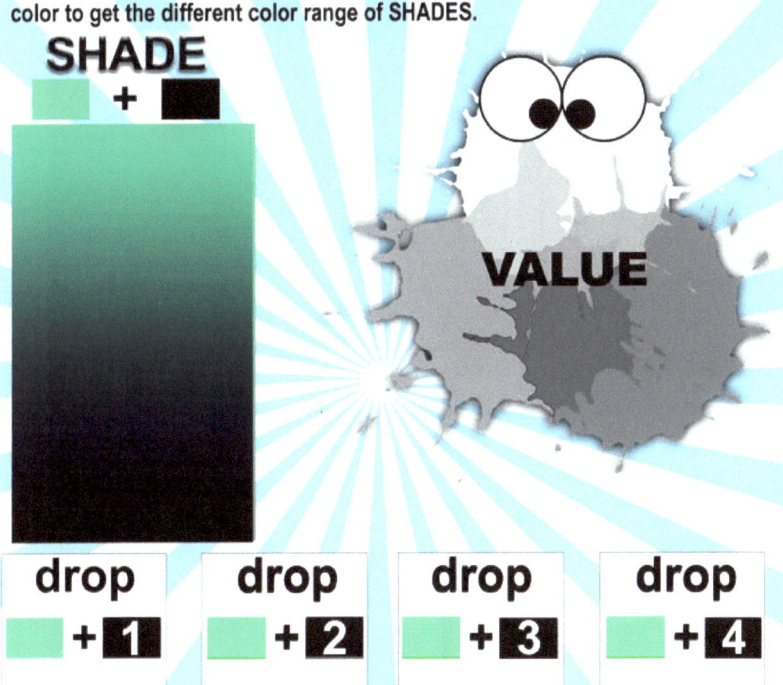

VALUE

| drop | drop | drop | drop |
|------|------|------|------|
| + 1 | + 2 | + 3 | + 4 |

43

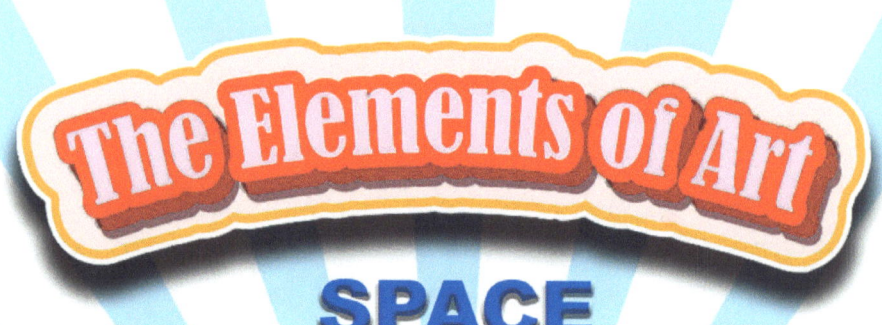

# SPACE

**Draw a flower vase in the box below and show Positive space and Negative space.**

**Example**

**POSITIVE SPACE**
is the actual objects or shapes within an artwork

**NEGATIVE SPACE**
is the space around and between those objects.

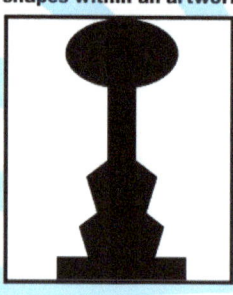 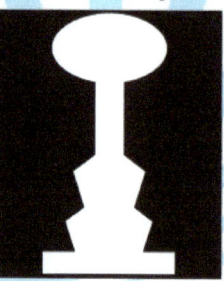

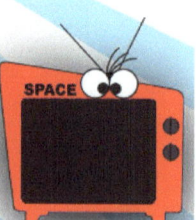

44

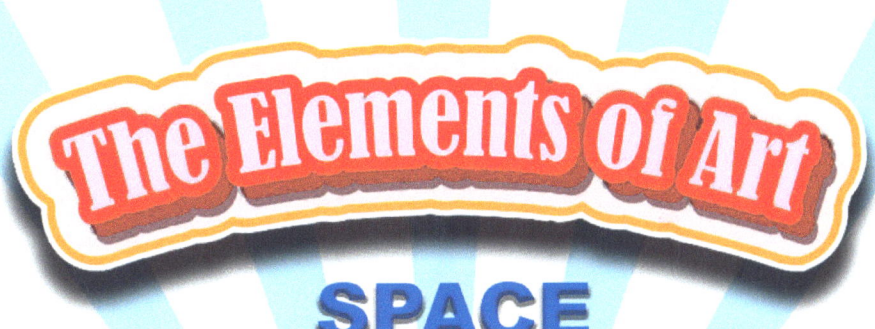

# SPACE

**SPACE is the distance and the area around and within shapes, forms, colors and lines. Space can be positive or negative. It includes the background, foreground and middle ground.**

## POSITIVE SPACE

is the actual objects or shapes within an artwork

## NEGATIVE SPACE

is the space around and between those objects.

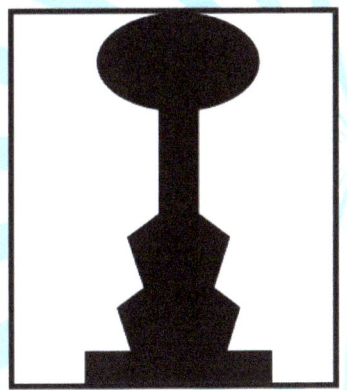

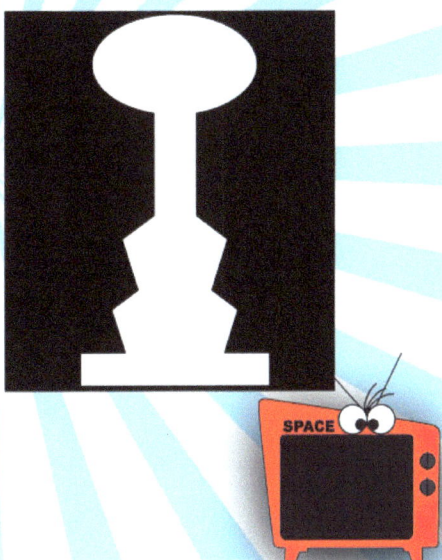

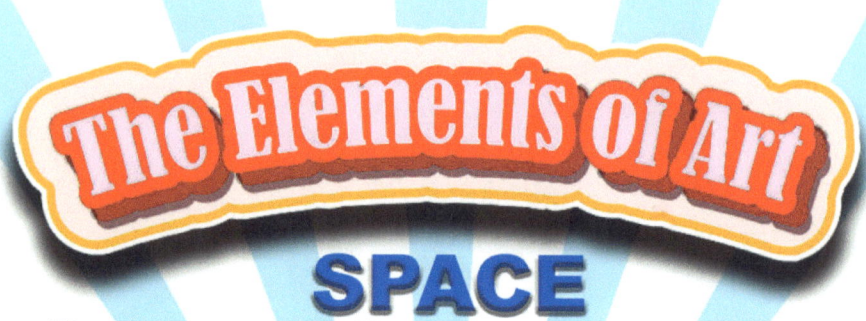

# SPACE

We also can create an illusion of space on a 2D artwork. There are six ways an artist can create the illusion of space on a 2-Dimensional surface.

**Overlapping** - when objects that are closer to the viewer prevent the view of objects that are behind them.

**Placement on the paper** - Objects placed higher within the picture plane will appear further away.

**Size** - Objects that are smaller will appear further away from the viewer.

**Detail** - Objects that are further away should have less detail than objects that are closer to the viewer.

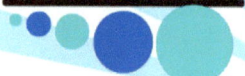

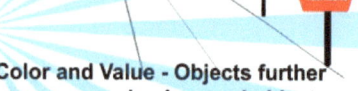

**Color and Value** - Objects that are further away are lighter color value, while objects that are closer are darker value.

**Color and Value** - Objects further away are cool colors and objects that are closer are warm colors.

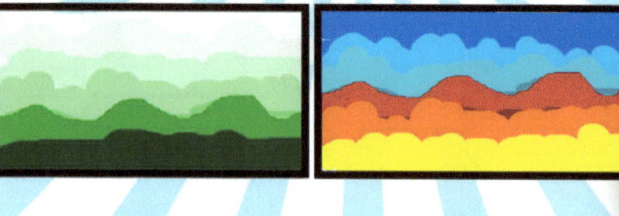

https://thevirtualinstructor.com/space.html

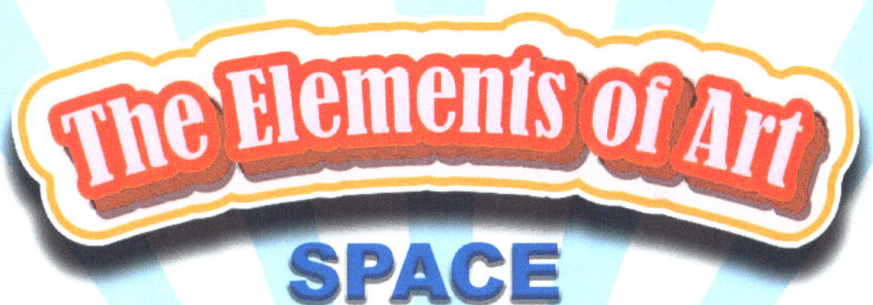

# SPACE

**Critique the watercolor picture below and make notations about the use of elements.**

Are there variations of shapes? Notice the use of complementary colors. What are they?
Are there shadows in the picture and where do you think the light is coming from?
Is there a variation of size in the subject matter?
Identify horizontal, vertical, curvy, and diagonal lines used in the picture.
Does the color value diminish as you recede into the distance?
Is there positive and negative space in the picture?

A resource in understanding the vocabulary used above
can be found on (artglossaryabout.comhome)

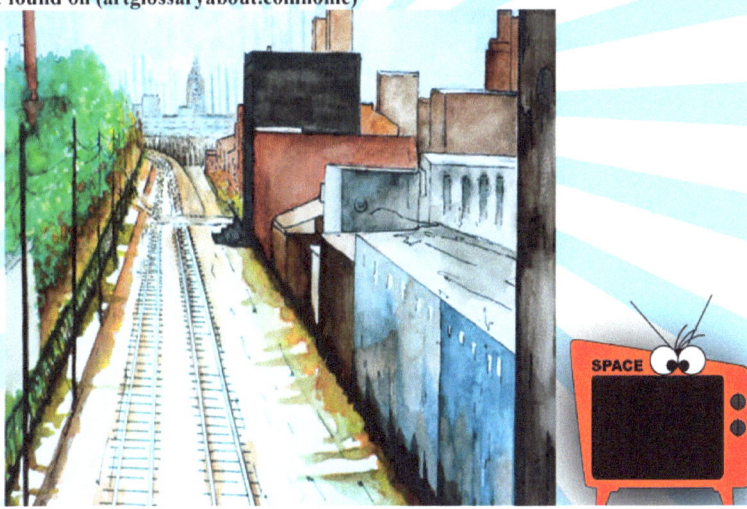

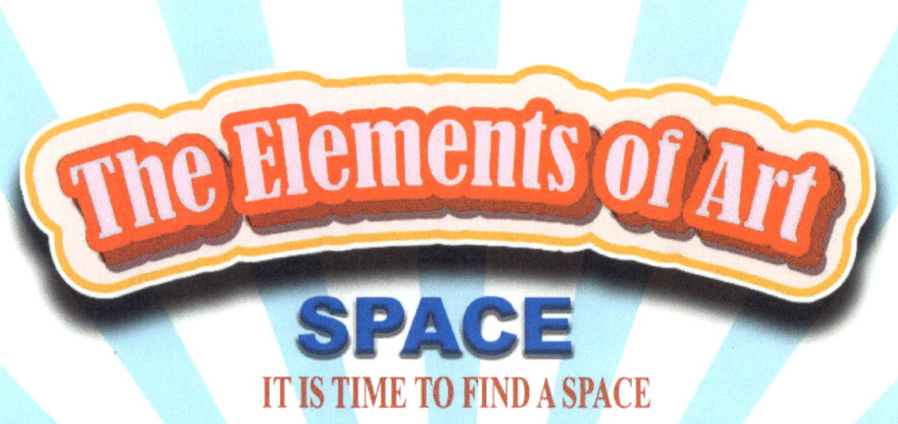

## SPACE

IT IS TIME TO FIND A SPACE

CHOOSE A MEDIUM
CHOOSE A SUBJECT MATTER
MAKE A QUICK SKETCH
WHERE WILL YOU PLACE YOUR OBJECTS?
WHAT COLORS WILL YOU USE?
WILL YOUR SUBJECT HAVE TEXTURE?
MAKE MISTAKES!
REMEMBER POSITIVE AND NEGATIVE SPACE
WILL THERE BE A HORIZON LINE?
WILL THERE BE A VANISHING POINT?
WILL THERE BE A FOREGROUND?
A MIDDLE GROUND?
A BACKGROUND?

HAPPY CREATING OR CRITIQUING!

SPACE

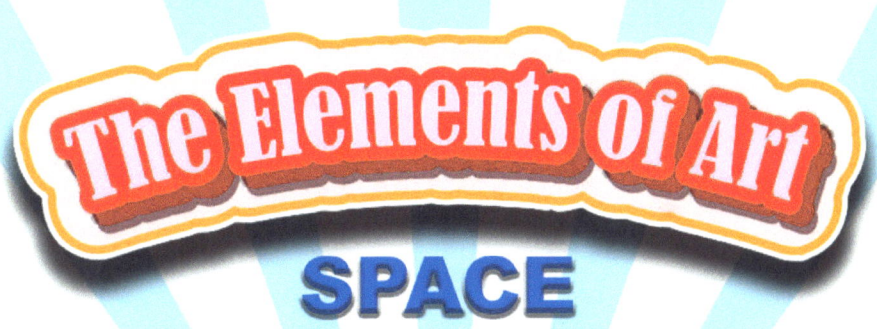

# SPACE

**A FOREGROUND, A MIDDLE GROUND, BACKGROUND AND IN-BETWEEN**

**IN THE PAINTING BELOW IS THERE A FOREGROUND, MIDDLE AND BACKGROUND?**
**THE LAMP POST AND CLOCK AS FOREGROUND SUBJECTS? WHAT SUBJECT MATTER IS IN THE BACKGROUND? THE SKY, TREES, AND FLOWERS AS THE IN-BETWEEN? THE CURB AND SIDEWALK AS FOREGROUND?**

**CRITIQUE AND MAKE NOTATIONS**

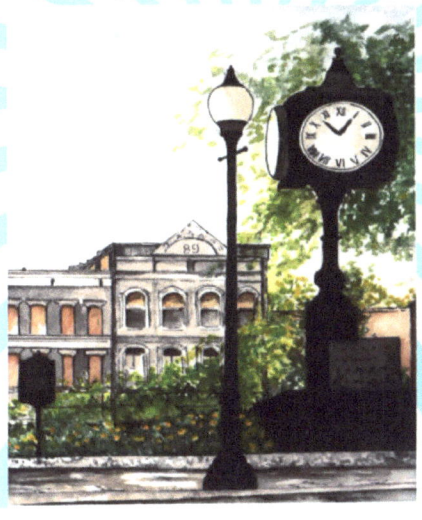

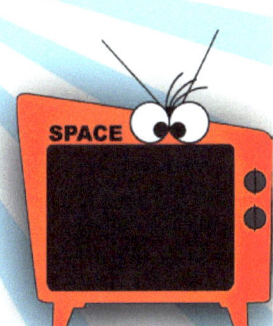

# REFERENCE LIST

https://thevirtualinstructor.com/space.html
https://en.wikipedia.org/wiki/Elements_of_art

## The Elements of Art
## Katherine "Kem" Kowa

www.ingramcontent.com/pod-product-compliance
Lightning Source LLC
Chambersburg PA
CBHW041106180526
45172CB00001B/139